A.E.R. — DEC 1975.

Mathematics in secondary schools – a teaching approach

Mathematics in Secondary Schools – a Teaching Approach

P. G. SCOPES
Principal Lecturer and Head of Mathematics Department
Avery Hill College of Education, London

Cambridge
at the University Press
1973

Published by the Syndics of the Cambridge University Press
Bentley House, 200 Euston Road, London NW1 2DB
American Branch: 32 East 57th Street, New York, N.Y. 10022

© Cambridge University Press 1973

Library of Congress Catalogue Card Number: 72–78894

ISBNs
0 521 08645 0 hard covers
0 521 09728 6 paperback

Photoset and printed in Malta,
by St Paul's Press Ltd.

Contents

Introduction   *page* vii

1 *The Teaching Process*   1
   Goals; objectives; content; strategy; method; materials; evaluation.

2 *The Goals of Education*   6
   Utilitarian goals   6
   Social goals   7
   Cultural goals   8
   Personal goals   8

3 *Defining the Objectives of Teaching Mathematics*   11
   Mathematics in everyday life and as a tool for other subjects.   11
   Methods of investigation: scientific, intuitive, deductive, and inventive. 12
   The history of mathematics and the development of mathematical
   thought.   15
   Mathematics as a language, and aspects of 'translation'.   16
   Beauty in mathematics   18
   Summary   19

4 *The Content of the Course*   21
   Modern aspects of content   21
       Sets – and number theory, geometry, relations, statistics and
   logic; flow charts and computers; modern approaches to problem
   solving.
   Traditional aspects of content   41
       Measurement; drawing three dimensional objects; the triangle;
   the circle and sphere; methods of calculation; basic algebra; graph work;
   Euclidean geometry.
   Summary of content   58
   Organising the subject material   60
       A statement of the problem; analysis of course work in the School
   Mathematics Project; analysis of course work in *Making mathematics*.
   Overall Summary   70

5 *Strategy*   72
   Differences in student ability and ways of meeting the problem.   72
       Variation of assignment; 'enrichment topics'; the use of work
   cards; programmed texts.
   Different learning processes   77
       The investigation; problem solving; forming concepts; learning
   skills; the place of memory work.

v

Controlling progress   87
Different approaches to selected topics   88
    Multiplication of directed numbers; simultaneous linear
equations; Pythagoras' theorem; trigonometry; logarithms.
The instructional file   105
Summary   106

6 *Method*   107
    The Scheme of work   107
    Unit plans   108
    The daily lesson plan   109
    Types of lesson   110
    Full class lessons; group lessons; individualised lessons;
broadcast lessons; films; games; visiting speakers; field trips;
introducing a new topic; consolidation; student directed class
discussion; practical lessons; problem solving; the communication
lesson.
    Classroom organisation   122
    Summary   123

7 *Materials*   124
    Commercially produced aids   124
    Motion picture films; filmstrips; television; tape recorders; 8 mm
film loop cassettes; overhead projector; opaque projector; charts, maps,
and graphs; display boards; blackboards; structured apparatus.
    Teacher produced aids in various situations
    Finite arithmetics; signed numbers; solid geometry; latitude and
longitude; plans and elevations; transformation geometry; curve stitching;
games.
    Measuring equipment   143
    Aids to computation   144
    The Mathematics Laboratory   147
    The Mathematics Library   149
    Summary   150

8 *Evaluation*   151
    Everyday evaluation   151
    The 'profile' as a means of assessment   153
    Written exercises and the teacher's record   154
    Types of test and how to set them   157
    Desirable features of all tests – validity, reliability, fairness,
discrimination, being comprehensive; ease of administration and
scoring.
    The heirarchy of the 'cognitive domain'   162
    Analysis of examination papers.   166
    Summary   173

Appendix.   The Mathematics Laboratory   174

Introduction

A lot has been said and written recently about 'Modern Mathematics'. The word, 'modern' in this context is used in two quite distinct ways. The first of these refers to actual changes of *content* in the curriculum to bring the mathematics of the classroom up to date and to make people aware of some of the developments in mathematics over the past 200 years. In particular there have been very profound changes in approaches to geometry and to algebraic structures. The influence of statistical methods on a side variety of subjects has also made itself felt, and in more recent times still the advent of the computer is having, and will continue to have, far-reaching repercussions not only on mathematics, but on our whole way of life.

However in addition to this modernising of the content of mathematics courses there has been another important change – a change in emphasis from methods of *teaching* to methods of *learning*. These 'new' methods emphasise *doing* as the most effective way of learning. The Nuffield Mathematics Project in Britain for example, has as the title of its first book, *I do and I understand*. It is significant, I think, that this is taken from part of an old Chinese proverb:

> I hear and I forget
> I see, and I remember
> I do, and I understand.

This shows us that, in fact, these methods are not *new* or *modern* at all, but have been employed by the best teachers right down through the centuries. They are only *new* to the extent that they are receiving far greater prominence and publicity than they did in the past.

Many of the 'Modern Mathematics' textbooks at the Secondary level have in their Teachers' Guides very full and extensive notes on the mathematical content, structure and reasons for inclusion of the new material that they contain. But, by and large, they don't give much help in this matter of classroom technique, and of new methods of organisation and approach which so many teachers feel they need.

This situation is in marked contrast to that in Primary Schools where there are numerous books on approach, technique, method and very little on the *mathematical reasons* for the inclusion of various topics. There is in some cases a distinct danger of activity for the sake of activity.

As is nearly always the case, a compromise course has to be set drawing on the best of both extremes, and the hope that I have for this book is that it will draw together strands from both aspects of the 'New Mathematics' and present them in a coherent, logical and useful form for the practising teacher.

But this can only be a start. Every teacher must make the attempt to keep himself up to date, to discuss new ideas and approaches, to initiate new work himself. It is of enormous value to associate oneself with a professional organisation both on a country-wide and on a local basis, and to receive and read material regularly which relates to one's work, such as the Association of Teachers of Mathematics publication *Mathematics teaching*. In this way one continues to grow, and this stimulus is transferred to one's pupils who, seeing a lively and responsive teacher, find inspiration and enjoyment in mathematics themselves.

Acknowledgement

Thanks are due to the Mathematical Association for permission to reproduce a diagram and material in the appendix from their pamphlet on Mathematics Laboratories in Schools, and to the Associated Examining Board for the General Certificate of Education for permission to include an extract of an O-level examination paper.

1. The Teaching Process

We, as teachers, are concerned with educating children. This process of education goes on all the time, at school, at home, and when we are relaxing. It is influenced by environment, by people, by physical and emotional problems, and by a lot of other experiences which often seem haphazard and uncontrolled. Yet in the school, the situation is more carefully organised. In school, we try to influence the development of individual children along particular lines. Our attempts are characterised by the term, 'teaching'.

Many these days would say that the emphasis is no longer so much on 'teaching by the teacher' as on 'learning by the learner'. This is merely a change in emphasis within the school; an attempt to make the process of education more efficient. In so far as this is a deliberate choice, it may be regarded as a teaching technique, for it is the teacher who makes the decision, and it is the teacher who sets up the environment within the school.

The teaching process may be summarised as in the flow-chart (Fig. 1). A brief account is given here which will be developed in subsequent chapters of this book.

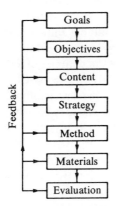

Fig. 1.

The starting point is the establishment of *goals*, or the defining of policy. What is the school trying to achieve? And within these broad educational goals, what are we trying to achieve in the time

1

allocated to mathematics? It is essential that we keep referring back to these fundamental priorities. It is very easy later on to get so involved in the details of actual teaching that we lose sight of the larger aims which should always occupy the first place. For example we might spend a lot of time considering more and more efficient ways of teaching children how to find the square root of a number, when with the pupils concerned this whole *activity* is educationally unimportant, or even positively detrimental.

To attain the general goals of which we have spoken we need next to define more specific *objectives* for our work in mathematics. In order to do this we have to be fairly clear as to the importance of mathematics to society at large. We also need to consider the part that mathematics plays in the overall education of the individual. These objectives will probably be broken down into three main categories:

(i)   Skills: what we hope children will be able to do.
(ii) Concepts: what we hope children will come to know and understand.
(iii) Attitudes: how we hope children will feel towards mathematics, and how they will react in different situations.

These objectives should be stated in terms of desired behaviour, for it is the student's behaviour which will finally indicate his achievement of these objectives.

The next step is the selection of appropriate *content*. This is one of the chief areas of contention between *traditional* and *modern* courses. One of the chief criteria for choice seems to me to be whether the inclusion of a topic serves as a 'unifying' influence in the understanding of mathematics, or as a 'growing point' for further development. The culmination of this stage is the defining of a curriculum, or the outlining of a course. Frequently in the past teachers have been placed in a situation in which the curriculum has already been described, the objectives defined, and they have not felt free to query it. This is hardly likely to be the case any more. Questions are now constantly being asked as to the purpose and place of every form of educational activity, and in the enquiry Mathematics must take its place. So every teacher needs, for his own satisfaction, to be able to say *why* any particular topic is included, for *whom* it is appropriate, and in *what way* it can best be presented. Only then can he really teach the subject with wisdom and authority.

For each section of work now decided upon as suitable *content* for a course we need to determine an appropriate *strategy* or *ap-*

proach. This will depend on the nature of the topic itself, the class in our care, the overall objectives which we must constantly keep in mind, and known procedures, aids, classroom techniques with which we are familiar and in which we are competent. As an example let us consider some possible strategies in approaching the addition of signed numbers. We will assume that preliminary work on the allocation of signs $+$ and $-$ to indicate opposites has been done.

(1) Consider a store-keeper who has a number of sacks of grain (e.g. rice, maize or millet) whose weights are all recorded as comparisons with a *standard* sack. $+3$ thus indicates a sack whose weight is 3 units *more* than the standard weight. -5 indicates a sack whose weight is 5 units *less* than the standard weight. Addition is then the putting together of two or more sacks. What then is the overall position when we have two sacks:

(a) $+3 + {}^{+}4$?
(b) $-2 + {}^{-}5$? etc.

(2) Steps right are considered as positive, steps left as negative. Addition, indicated by $+$, really means 'and then', so $+3 + {}^{+}2$ means 3 steps right *and then* 2 steps right. Altogether?

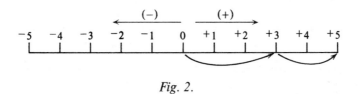

Fig. 2.

Similarly for other combinations.

(3) Two scales are provided (Fig. 3). To add, put the *zero* of the *A* scale on *top of the first number* on the *B* scale.

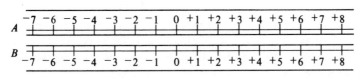

Fig. 3.

Fig. 4 shows the scales set for $+3 + x$.

3

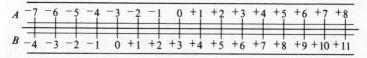

Fig. 4.

Now find the second number of the A scale, and read down. Thus
$^+3 + {}^+2 = {}^+5;$ $^+3 + {}^-4 = {}^-1;$ $^+3 + {}^-3 = 0$ etc.

(4) Ordered pairs of natural numbers are partitioned into sets so that in any given set the difference between the first and second members of the ordered pair is constant. These sets are named by that common difference.

So $^+3 = \{(0, 3), (1, 4), (2, 5) \ldots\}$

Likewise $^-2 = \{(2, 0), (3, 1), (4, 2) \ldots\}$

Notice that the *order* of the members is very significant. Addition is defined by choosing any member of the first set and any member of the second set and forming the sums of the first terms and of the second terms of the ordered pairs chosen, and finding what set this belongs to.

Thus $^+3 + {}^-2$ is found by considering, say

$(1, 4) + (4, 2) = (5, 6)$

or $(2, 5) + (5, 3) = (7, 8)$ Note that all the resulting ordered

or $(0, 3) + (5, 3) = (5, 6)$ pairs belong to the set labelled

or   . . . . $^+1$. So we say $^+3 + {}^-2 = {}^+1$

Closely related to considerations of *strategy* come considerations of *method* and of *materials*. Each of the strategies above could be developed by a straightforward, conventional lesson with the teacher talking to whose class and using the blackboard. But we could use other means, for example work cards, or group discussion. Or we might decide to have four groups and use a different plan with each group. Later we could rotate round so that each group gets experience of each approach. Alternatively we may find that one or more of these approaches is well developed in a textbook or elsewhere and so be able to assign work individually. There may also be film strips or films which illustrate one or more of these approaches. Which method we eventually choose also depends on a number of factors such as the background of the pupils and the work they have done before.

The final step in teaching is to evaluate the work done by yourself as teacher and the level of understanding and attainment reached by your students. This can also be done in a variety of ways – by tests, by exercises, by written work, by project work involving the new concepts, by discussion and so on. What you find out will affect the previous steps in the process so that changes are made when you revise or when you teach the same topic again. In this sense the work of a teacher is never done. There must be constant evaluation, self-criticism, search for improvement.

Remember this brief outline of the teaching process as we approach the other parts of this book. In them we will try to explain in more detail each of the various steps mentioned here.

2. The Goals of Education

The start of the proper practice of education and of teaching is an understanding of the purpose of the whole educational system, and what it aims at. These aims, of course, are always subject to change. To quote Jerome S. Bruner: 'I shall take it as self-evident that each generation must define afresh the nature, direction and aims of education to assure such freedom and rationality as can be attained for a future generation.' [*Toward a theory of instruction.* Cambridge, Mass. Harvard University Press, 1966, p. 22.]

In a book of this kind which is related specifically to the teaching of Mathematics in a variety of situations where the educational policies may be markedly different, we shall have to confine ourselves to those aims which are seen to obtain generally. However, in any specific situation there will be other important factors which will affect the issue.

We may usefully divide the goals of education under a number of subheadings as Fig. 5.

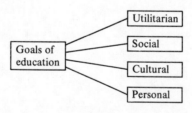

Fig. 5.

Utilitarian goals
These are really at two levels, those of the state and those of the individual. From the state's point of view, education is a resource, and often an expensive one, from which certain returns can and should be expected. The educational system must therefore provide sufficient numbers of trained professional people of every kind to meet the requirements of the country in its own continuing existence and development. In many countries this aspect of 'man-power planning' is central both to educational thought and practice and to the overall economic programme which may be spelled out in a

6

Five Year or Ten Year Plan. Clearly the place of the secondary schools in this development is crucial, and the requirements by subjects for certain numbers of candidates may be very specific indeed. There are, however, certain inherent dangers in such policies, as those 'selected' for certain types of work or education may feel themselves 'set apart', an elite divorced from the 'common man' and deserving of special attention and special privileges. This is a danger that must be acknowledged, but counter-balanced by providing adequate social goals which are discussed below.

Apart, however, from the need for people to do a number of specific jobs, there are certain practical or utilitarian skills that can be expected of all school leavers. Amongst these are the ability to read and write and to do a minimum amount of mathematics. In the next chapter we consider just what this minimum amount should be.

Social goals
Besides utilitarian skills, society requires of the school leaver much more. It expects that, throughout his time at school, the child is made aware of himself in relation to other people. This includes, of course, his immediate family, the school community, the somewhat larger local community and various societies and organizations. He also should come to see himself as a citizen of his country, and as a human being with certain rights. These rights, however, carry with them responsibilities, and require an attitude of understanding and concern for other people.

Thus the whole business of character training must be amongst the educational aims of any society. Children must be brought up to see that they form part of society, that they have a part to play, but that this part may be very different for different people. This is true whatever country a child is brought up in. Within the community of that land there will be people with many different kinds of jobs. All these people depend on each other, and no-one can claim to be more important than everyone else.

Moreover in order to have rights, people must accept responsibilities; and in order to gain certain freedoms, people must be prepared to fore-go other freedoms, and to expect and accept laws and rules which society can enforce. In addition to this, when a country is going through a period of rapid change, it is essential that people should recognize the importance of continuity and of tradition, for each of us is dependent on those who have gone before. This leads us next to consider cultural goals.

7

Cultural goals

Every society has its own culture, and part of the duty of education is to make young people aware of the strengths and virtues of the culture they have inherited. Foremost in this realm will be the study of language and literature. So where reading and writing are strictly utilitarian goals, they should pass on to the refinements of literature and speech, of poetry and art. Language, it will be learned, serves many purposes – local conversation, the dissemination of knowledge, the art of persuasion and of logical inference, the structure of thought, the raising of emotions, the description of events and places, and the means of expressing thoughts and feelings ranging from the ridiculous to the sublime.

Much of the culture of a country is also enshrined in its history, and clearly some knowledge of the history of one's country is something one can expect from any secondary school leaver. This study of history will reveal the inner motivations of men through the centuries; it will touch on values to be honoured and those to be deplored; it will show how change has been brought about – by revolution, and by evolution – and it will try to set the state for present government policies whether these be for consolidation or change. There will be, in addition, an exploration of other creative fields such as art, architecture and music.

Personal goals

These goals relate to the proper development of the innate abilities of each individual for *his own sake*, to help him lead a rich life, to enable him to enjoy life and to find pleasure in a variety of activities. All this requires the recognition of each person as an individual in his own right, distinct, separate, and valuable for himself. This view springs sometimes from religious considerations, the idea of each person as a child of God, and as such a creation of infinite value. Those who do not claim a religious affiliation, however, still maintain passionately the goals of full self-expression, for they say, it is only as each individual realises his potentialities that he finds satisfaction, and it is only the satisfied who can live harmoniously with others.

The implications of these views are considerable for they demand giving *opportunities* for individuals to embark on a wide variety of experience – to develop potentials of body, mind, and spirit; to create an environment in which the bodily physique is properly developed, where health is the normal state; to provide experiences

8

in music and art, and in every realm of aesthetic appreciation so that those who can, do develop both their awareness of values, and their ability to express themselves in these ways; and to ensure that religion is not side-tracked since the development of the soul and mystic regeneration is as valid a human experience as any other. Such provision must include corporate activity of large groups all together, in team games, in music and dance, in films and theatrical productions, and in services of worship. It must also, however, include the chance for individual development and practice, for withdrawal from the main group to pursue an individual interest, and to develop a personal commitment and skill.

The statements above are an attempt to define an ideal towards which any educational system should work. Two other points, however should be made:

(1) that no educational system can in itself achieve all the aims it sets out to achieve if it has not got the sympathetic backing and support of the community at large, and

(2) that because of the enormous variety of individual abilities, as well as considerations of sheer economics, the relative emphases we put on each of these goals will vary. That all four strands are necessary, I think perhaps no-one would deny; of their relative importance for different categories of child there will always be deep argument.

Nevertheless it is my contention that in *any* school situation, every one of the goals mentioned above must be kept in mind. It may well be that for the very able, a great deal more time and effort can be given to cultural aims, the development of intellectual disciplines, and the acquiring of complex skills and appreciations, the chance for each student to pursue his own interests at his own speed and along lines that others may not follow at all. For the low achiever, not so much time can be given to these aspects, but it is fatal to omit them altogether; for it is in accepting and overcoming challenges both mental and physical that are within his capability that a person develops self-confidence. There is often a tendency to emasculate the overall aims for such children by giving courses which consist entirely of *basic skills*, or to meet only what are thought to be *vocational* (i.e. employment) needs. Whenever this is done we destroy any chance of developing positive attitudes. Instead a programme is needed, which if limited, is sound, is significant for the learner and is within range of his capacity.

In the same way in developing countries it is clear that social and national considerations will play a much more important relative part than in developed countries like England whose identity has been established for centuries. But it would be fatal if this were to result in a conformity which did not allow for individual expression and initiative. On the other hand in England there is at present a very considerable danger that the cult of self-expression has been over-emphasised to the neglect of social and national concerns. It is only as a proper *balance* is achieved that a sound educational pattern can be found.

3. Defining the Objectives of Teaching Mathematics

In the previous chapter a very brief account was given of the goals of education under the headings: utilitarian goals, social goals, cultural goals, and personal goals. In this chapter we will consider the more specific role of mathematics in each of these.

The utilitarian goals are the most obvious and because they are the most obvious they often assume too large a part of the overall objectives we keep before us. Every person, on leaving school, should have clear ideas of number, and a comprehension of both the very large and the very small. He should understand the way number is applied to measures of all varieties, but most particularly to those physical concepts he meets with most frequently – length, volume, weight, area, density, temperature, speed, acceleration, and pressure. His knowledge of such measures should not be just academic, but also practical so that he can estimate realistically employing the standard measures of the community. Increasingly this means in the future a fundamental appreciation of the size of various metric measures. He should be able to use correctly, accurately, and with understanding the four fundamental operations of addition, subtraction, multiplication and division as applied both to number and to measurement, and be able to check both his own and other people's calculations by appropriate approximation.

He should have experience of representing three dimensional objects on a flat piece of paper by a variety of techniques, and understand the concepts of ratio and of scale drawing. He should be able to read and interpret graphs, diagrams and tables, particularly those relating to statistical evidence, and should be aware of devices whereby statistics can be used to mislead rather than to enlighten! He should recognize too that graphs are frequently a convenient and powerful way of representing relations and, as such, play an important role in the discovery of such relations. Lastly he should be able to apply his knowledge of mathematics to a wide range of problems that continually occur in his everyday life.

These are utilitarian goals for *every* citizen in the world today.

However the list of topics for inclusion rises dramatically if we begin to think of mathematics as a tool for specialised occupations like science, engineering, economics, and computing. Then basic algebra, calculus, trigonometry, statistics, to mention but a few, are considered as *essential* background. Schools must make provision for *some* students to include all these aspects whilst ensuring that every student has a basic course in mathematics covering the fundamentals outlined above.

However, it must be stressed again that if we allowed utilitarian goals to dominate our thinking we would be doing both society and the individual student a gross disservice. Mathematics has far more to offer. One of the aims of education rather crudely put earlier was 'To help the child lead a rich life'. A rich life includes within it a number of ingredients of which the most important are the following: firstly *success*, for success instils confidence, and confidence an attitude of concern for, and interest in things round about. This interest will be informed by a sense of values which contrasts strongly with the aimless drifting of the uncommitted who can see no value in any of the activities that society can offer. But a person leading a rich life has a wide variety of interests and activities, social, cultural, intellectual, recreational, creative. And in every one of these directions mathematics can contribute!

Mathematics properly approached and organised can give moments of success to everyone, the satisfaction of mastering a skill, or the pleasure of combining with others to present a discovery to a wider audience. It can help to build social values in projects corporately undertaken; it so runs through the whole of our culture, in art, music, language, logic, and science that it is virtually impossible to do without it; in intellectual pursuits it stands amongst the foremost accomplishments of the human mind; mathematical games and puzzles provide a life-long avenue of recreation; and finally to some it provides a source of creative inspiration at least as valid as that provided by artistic pursuits to others.

Utilitarian goals, therefore, are far too narrow to represent the total reason for including mathematics in any course, and any course that does so constrict its objectives is inevitably flat, barren, uninspired, and frequently has, as its outcome, pupils who detest and loathe mathematics as a subject.

Let us turn then to the social goals. Students need to understand how mathematics' methods are used to investigate, interpret, and to make decisions in human affairs, and how mathematics contributes to his understanding of natural phenomena. These methods may be

12

summarised in four words, scientific, intuitive, deductive, and inventive, and ideally each should be present in any overall programme of mathematics teaching.

The *scientific method* is that in which one seeks to discover order, pattern and relations, not only in the man-made world, but in the natural world as well. These patterns may relate simply to different sets of numbers as in the study of series, or they may relate to sets of quantities·or measures, e.g. increase in weight and extension of spring, length of pendulum and time of swing. Certainly the existence of pattern seems to imply a relationship and making such relationships explicit is one of the fundamental activities of mathematics.

Nowhere is this more evident than in the use of graphs. Indeed sometimes to make relations clearer we use special graph paper, as for example when studying polar co-ordinates, or logarithmic functions, or the 'normal distribution' in statistics. The discovery of a relation is immensely satisfying and to arrange circumstances so that as far as possible children discover (or re-discover) these for themselves is one of the most effective ways of improving attitudes towards mathematics.

The *intuitive method* is not so much a method as a recognition that frequently advances are made, not deliberately, consciously, step by step, but by a flash of insight, a sudden illumination of a concept, the jumping of a hurdle which brings understanding where none existed before. Such 'intuition' can be dangerous as mistakes can be made, and 'insights' can rest on misconceptions.

As a simple illustration of such dangers, consider the information displayed below:

$$2 \times 2 = 4 \qquad\qquad 2 + 2 = 4$$
$$\tfrac{3}{2} \times 3 = 4\tfrac{1}{2} \qquad\qquad \tfrac{3}{2} + 3 = 4\tfrac{1}{2}$$
$$\tfrac{4}{3} \times 4 = 5\tfrac{1}{3} \qquad\qquad \tfrac{4}{3} + 4 = 5\tfrac{1}{3}$$
$$\tfrac{5}{4} \times 5 = 6\tfrac{1}{4} \qquad\qquad \tfrac{5}{4} + 5 = 6\tfrac{1}{4}$$

A possible 'intuitive discovery' might be that the signs $\times$ and $+$ are interchangeable! That this is not a valid conclusion can be shown immediately by producing a counter-example, e.g.

$$2 \times 3 = 6 \qquad\qquad 2 + 3 = 5$$

However, a valid conclusion does exist, namely:

$$\frac{n}{n-1} \times n = (n+1) + \frac{1}{n-1} = \frac{n}{n-1} + n$$

That this is true can be confirmed by applying the processes of algebra to both the first and last terms and showing that each is equivalent to the middle term.

Thus our intuition must be linked closely with the third method, *deduction*. Here by working backwards as well as forwards, a whole chain of reasoning is established to link in a logically convincing way the results of one's insight or intuition to a framework that is mathematically acceptable.

Frequently of course, it is the final deductive process which is put on view and often while this is convincing, one is left with a sense of frustration and wonder – why did the writer proceed along these lines; they seem so far-fetched! Much more important to the mathematician is the *idea* that led to a particular avenue of exploration, or the development of a certain piece of work. This is frequently best done by reference to real problems, the solution of which require the idea in question. In trying to solve the problem, one becomes aware of the motivation which led to a given line of enquiry.

Lastly amongst the methods of mathematics lies the *inventive*. This inventiveness can relate to the defining of 'ideal' elements which have no *physical* reality but as a mathematical model represent the real world in all essential features. So in the elementary school we define a circle as a mathematical abstract of many commonly seen objects none of which *exactly* show the properties of a circle. Another such concept is that of infinity or that of a limit, a mathematical concept for which no physical counterpart is really adequate. This inventiveness relates too to providing a suitable symbolism, for a good symbolism will often suggest avenues of approach that are hidden if the symbolism is clumsy. An example of this is given on page 16 where one can see how effective the symbolism of Descartes is in comparison with those of previous mathematicians. Inventiveness arises also whenever we have a situation in which we feel intuitively there *ought* to be a solution but where we cannot find one within our present frame of reference. However, by extending this frame of reference, we *can* find solutions. So we trace the development of the idea of number from the set of natural numbers to that of integers, thence to rationals and reals, and in due course to the set of complex numbers.

It is important that students have the opportunity to make their own investigations, and that they should be encouraged in their work to produce something which shows all four of these methods.

14

So some investigations will involve the collation of facts, the organising of these facts in a meaningful way in tables, charts, diagrams, graphs, etc. and the interpreting of the data so arranged. More often than not some process of measurement will be involved, and this only seems natural. To quote Lord Kelvin: 'When you can measure what you are thinking about or when you can express it in numbers you know something about it; but when you cannot express it in numbers, your knowledge is of a meagre and unsatisfactory kind.' Other investigations will require intuition, deduction, and even inventiveness, particularly of suitable symbolism if students try to make clear what they have done for the benefit of others.

Besides the mathematical value of such investigations, there are other gains: the value of discussion, the value of co-operation, the acknowledgement that often several people working together can achieve results that none could have done individually. Students will learn the importance of organisation, the necessity to care for and maintain equipment so that it can be used by others, the virtue of putting things back in definite places so that they can be found again when required. In this way students will be led to an understanding of community rights as well as individual rights; they will learn to behave responsibly towards others. They will also learn that whereas competition is certainly *one* effective form of motivation, it is by no means the only one, nor necessarily the best. Frequently the best motivation of all is corporate endeavour in an occupation worthwhile on its own account.

We turn now to cultural goals, which in turn means that we must reflect for a moment on the part mathematics has played in the culture of the world of the past and continues to play in the culture of the world of today.

Every student should be made aware of some of the major strands in the history of mathematics, and how this has influenced the thought processes of successive generations. They should become aware of three aspects in the development of mathematical thought:

(1) Completely original thought processes which have revolutionised the thinking of the world. Amongst these were Thales' concept of proof, the invention of a symbol for zero, Descartes' idea of representing points in space by co-ordinates, the advent of the calculus, and in modern times the electronic computer.

(2) Development of techniques and a widening of the fields of both pure and applied mathematics. This is the role played by the new generation who stand on the shoulders of the giants of preced-

ing generations and apply their ideas to a wider field of activity.

(3) Inward-facing aspects where the foundations of mathematics are critically examined and the structure of mathematics thereby strengthened. The development in the last century of new geometries arising from a critical appraisal of the famous 'parallel postulate' of Euclid are examples of this type of work, and much of the current emphasis on *structure* in many modern mathematics programmes arises from work in this field.

Running parallel to these themes in the history of mathematics is the idea of communicating ideas, the whole concept of mathematics as a *language*. The language of mathematics is international for the symbols employed have an acceptance in many countries whose other languages of communication differ widely. Thus $3 + 4 = 7$ can be 'read' in English, French, German, Italian, Spanish, Swahili, etc. but in all these languages the statement is acceptable mathematically. In addition to its international character, mathematical symbolism well used, is a powerful creative force. That this is so can be seen in the way that an effective symbolism frees the mind to concentrate on essentials. Consider for example different ways of writing the same equation down through the ages:

Regiomontanus, A.D. 1464
> 3 Census et 6 demptis 5 rebus aequatur zero.

Pacioli, A.D. 1494
> 3 Census p. 6 de 5 rebus ae 0.

Vieta, A.D. 1591
> 3 in A quad − 5 in A plano + 6 aequatur 0.

Stevinus, A.D. 1585
> $3\textcircled{2} - 5\textcircled{1} + 6 = 0.$

Descartes, A.D. 1637
> $3x^2 - 5x + 6 = 0.$

[Lancelot Hogben: *Mathematics for the million*. London, George Allen and Unwin.]

Just how effective this final form is can be seen by trying to 'translate' the mathematical statement into English: 'If from the sum of six and the product of three and the square of an unknown quantity, the product of five and that same unknown quantity is subtracted, the result is zero.'! Clearly if we had to rely on English alone, further creative mathematical thinking would be impossible.

This business of 'translation' is fundamental to much of the utility of mathematics in the real world. Frequently the most difficult stage in solving a problem is finding the appropriate 'model'. In this sense a mathematical model is a construction which approximates to the real life situation. This often involves idealising that situation and neglecting certain 'irrelevant' features. For example, in many applications we represent the world as a perfect sphere, whereas we know that this is not strictly speaking the case. However, by considering the 'ideal' we are able to write equations which we can then solve by the techniques of mathematics. We then have to re-translate our mathematical solution into terms of real life and see whether this real life solution really does fit the original problem. We may represent the situation diagramatically, as in Fig. 6.

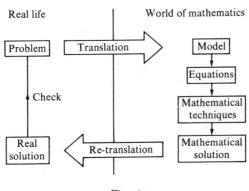

Fig. 6.

One of the most famous illustrations of this method is the celebrated Königsberg bridge problem, first solved by Euler in 1736. Königsberg is built where rivers join together, and there is an island in the main stream (see Fig. 7). The inhabitants used to try to walk over all of the seven bridges without retracing their steps or crossing any bridge more than once.

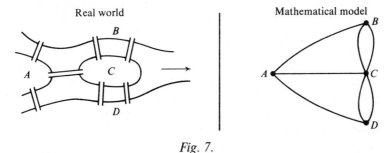

Fig. 7.

17

Euler changed the original problem into that shown by the mathematical model on the right, and rephrased the problem as being to outline the shape *unicursally*. He went on to show that to traverse any graph in this manner it must not have more than two *odd nodes*, i.e. meeting points with an odd number of branches. In such a case a solution is possible by starting at one of the odd nodes and finishing at the other. However in this graph there are *four* odd nodes and so the graph is multi-cursal. This shows that the inhabitants of Königsberg were wasting their time as no solution is possible. However, if *any one* bridge were removed the problem could easily be solved.

Another function of language, besides conveying meaning is persuading, and there is nothing more persuasive than logical argument. It is not surprising therefore, that another very important cultural aspect of mathematics is the examination of the whole idea of *logic*, and of the logical structure of mathematics, and the nature of proof. In any system of constructive thought the validity of the conclusions rests upon the *validity* and *consistency* of the assumptions and definitions upon which the conclusions are based. Distinctions need to be made between conclusions which *logically* result from a system of correct argument but possibly false premises, and of other results which are incorrectly drawn from premises which may be either true or false. Thus a feature of indirect proof is to consider a number of mutually exhaustive alternatives; to show that the *logical* consequences of all but one of these lead to a false conclusion, and thus assert the *truth* of the remaining alternative. This is the method frequently used by the hero in detective stories, who establishes the innocence of various parties one by one until the villain stands revealed as the only one without a cast-iron alibi.

And so we come to the last cultural objective, the sheer aesthetic fascination of mathematics. Initially this may be engendered by the contemplation of geometrical shapes, mosaics, solids, by symmetry, patterns which catch the eye; but ultimately it goes much deeper to appreciations of elegance in proof, of the effective use of symbolism, of the uniting of different branches of mathematics within a single overall embracing structure. Here is a realm as much the mathematician's own as that of the connoisseur of painting, or architecture, or music. If we can do anything at all to engender such appreciation in any of our pupils, we should!

This leads us directly to the last of the strands that appear in the general statement of goals – personal goals. We wish to develop in all students attitudes and appreciations which lead to curiosity, initiative and confidence, and to interests in various facets of mathematics. We want students to think for themselves. These aims, if accepted, demand a number of changes in many of the formal class activities that we are accustomed to. There must be opportunities for original work, both corporate and individual. Students must be challenged to tackle problems in a way that is both meaningful and productive. As they work they must learn how to use resource material, how to make use of the results of other people's work, how to tackle problems, when to look for help and when to persist on their own, how to assess the suitability of different mathematics models; how to ask pertinent questions; how to present material in a clear way so that it is fully intelligible to others. As they gain in experience they should gradually develop critical faculties, learn to look at their

UTILITARIAN GOALS	SOCIAL GOALS
(a) *Mathematics for everyday life* Number and number operations Measurement and approximation Basic geometry Graphs and relations	(a) *Methods of investigation* Scientific Intuitive Deductive Inventive
(b) *Tool for other subjects* Basic Algebra Calculus Trigonometry Statistics Vectors, matrices, etc.	(b) *Work with others* Organisation Care of equipment Community rights Social motivation
(c) *Foundation for further study* *in Mathematics for some*	

OBJECTIVES OF
MATHEMATICS
TEACHING

CULTURAL GOALS	PERSONAL GOALS
(a) *Historical developments* Original thought processes Developments based on these Examination of structure	(a) *Character building through* Active involvement Personal successes Work with others
(b) *Mathematics as a language* Shapes, size, and change The power of symbolism Mathematical models	(b) *Opportunities for stimulating* Curiosity Self-expression Self-criticism
(c) *Mathematics and LOGIC*	
(d) *Aesthetic appreciation*	

Fig. 8.

work objectively to see whether it represents the best of which they are capable. All this can be summarised as developing an attitude of *independence* within the overall framework of the social context in which they find themselves.

So called 'modern' mathematics puts this last strand of building up positive attitudes as the *primary goal* of teaching mathematics, for when a student's curiosity, concern, and creativeness are all aroused, learning becomes automatic. The point is that such motivation is *internal* and as such persists. It goes with an individual right through life. On the other hand knowledge accumulated as a result of outside pressures such as rewards, merits, and fear of failure is often lost as soon as those pressures are removed.

The substance of this chapter is summarised in Fig. 8. It needs to be stressed again and again that goals of all four varieties, those of attitude, utility, social development and cultural background, should be present in any course of mathematics with any group of children; and that any course that omits any one of these is likely to fail. We must recognise that any child leaving the educational system who is not employable, or is not a good citizen, or who has developed no interests, no awareness of cultural values, or has no confidence in any of his abilities, represents a loss to society at large, and a failure of the educational system in particular.

4. The Content of the Course

Having considered the objectives of teaching mathematics in the secondary school we can turn to the question of the content of the course, and the allied question, the organisation of that content. For any teacher knows that though a *syllabus* is a necessary first consideration, there remains the very important question as to how that syllabus should be organised in order to be most efficiently taught, or from the learner's point of view, most successfully learned.

In the early part of this chapter we shall consider the question of *what* to include, or the actual *content*. Naturally this account is bound to be very condensed and only the main points can be included. For full expositions of content one must turn to text-books themselves or to books designed with this particular purpose in mind. Our concern here is how content relates to teaching.

In the second part of this chapter we shall look at some of the criteria for ordering this material in the most satisfactory way. Evidence from a number of sources indicates that topics are more easily learned if they form an integral part of an overall *scheme*. The features of such a scheme are that material is revised, looked at from different points of view, related to other aspects of work, and so kept constantly in mind. So we shall examine the main threads that should run through a secondary school course, turning our attention first to those topics which feature heavily in *modern* mathematics courses, and then come back to consider themes from traditional courses which are still necessary.

Sets
The first of these threads, and probably the most important, is the idea of *sets*. Just how fundamental sets are can be seen by looking at Fig. 9. This illustrates *some* of the more important directions and applications that spring from a basic understanding of sets. Let us look at each of these strands in slightly more detail.

Sets and number theory
Our understanding of number springs from experience with sets and the basic operation of 'matching' or of 'one-to-one correspondence'.

22

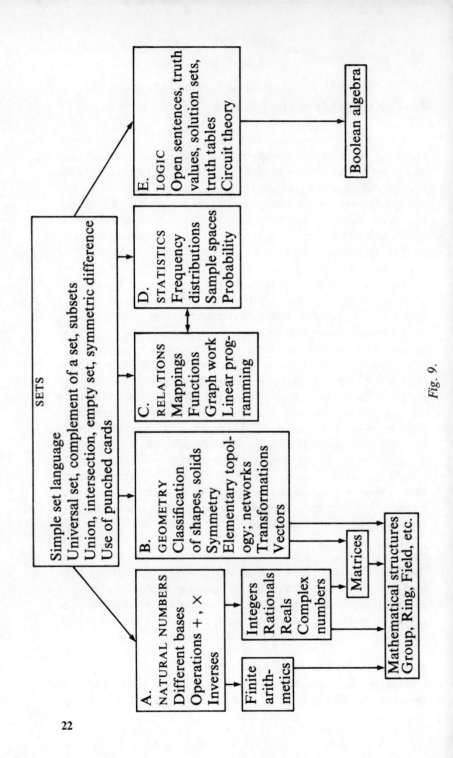

SETS
Simple set language
Universal set, complement of a set, subsets
Union, intersection, empty set, symmetric difference
Use of punched cards

A.
NATURAL NUMBERS
Different bases
Operations $+$, $\times$
Inverses

Finite arithmetics

Integers
Rationals
Reals
Complex numbers

Matrices

Mathematical structures
Group, Ring, Field, etc.

B.
GEOMETRY
Classification of shapes, solids
Symmetry
Elementary topology; networks
Transformations
Vectors

C.
RELATIONS
Mappings
Functions
Graph work
Linear programming

D.
STATISTICS
Frequency distributions
Sample spaces
Probability

E.
LOGIC
Open sentences, truth values, solution sets, truth tables
Circuit theory

Boolean algebra

Fig. 9.

Sets which match are said to be *equivalent* or to have the same number of members or elements.

This is our first introduction to equivalence, but the idea is of much wider application. It arises whenever there is some property of *alikeness* that can be abstracted; some sense of sameness. The quality of sameness that strikes us, however, depends on what we want to *do* with the set, and so we are led next to consider various operations. The most basic numerical operation is addition.

When this operation is applied to members of the set of natural numbers we discover that the result is always another member of the same set. In other words if a and b are natural numbers, and $a + b = c$, c is also a natural number. We may well now want to ask, 'If a and c are natural numbers, and $a + b = c$, is b also a natural number?' We find that it is provided that c is greater than a. This restriction, however, is irksome, and so we are led to extend our set of natural numbers to include 'negative' numbers and zero, and thus form the set of integers.

With the establishment of a second operation, multiplication, progress along exactly similar lines leads us to define another new kind of number, the *rational* number (i.e. one that can be expressed in the form of a ratio). The way is now open for a new kind of *equivalence*, the equivalence of two fractions. So we say that $\frac{1}{2}$, $\frac{2}{4}$, $\frac{3}{6}$, $\frac{4}{8}$, $\frac{5}{10}$, ... are all *equivalent* fractions, that is the *same for purposes of numerical calculation*. In other respects, of course, they are different. For example, although we write $\frac{1}{2} = \frac{8}{16}$, a half a loaf of bread will produce very different physical impressions than will 8 equal slices which make up half a loaf.

It will be noticed that positive rationals are made up of two numbers, each of which separately is drawn from the set of natural numbers, and that we could equally well refer to the fraction a/b as an ordered pair (a, b), or indeed (b, a) if we used a different definition. In either case we would have to give suitable definitions for equivalence and for the operations of addition and multiplication to be consistent with our previous use of these terms.

So *equivalence* is largely a matter of definition, but it occurs repeatedly in our progress in number theory from rationals, to reals, to complex numbers. It turns up again in our use of vectors, in finite arithmetics in any modulus, in transformation geometry, in matrix algebra. In every case there is a *sameness* which we recognise, abstract define, and use. A most concise and useful survey of the notion of equivalence in the context of school mathematics has been written by

23

D. A. Quadling and published for the Mathematical Association by George Bell, London under the title, *The same but different*.

The idea of *operations* in different connections leads us on to consider *structure*, and again to notice certain likenesses. The simplest of these structures is the group. A group is a set of elements, $a, b, \ldots$ which can be combined by an operation $*$ which exhibits the following properties:

(1) *Closure*: The result $a * b$ of combining any two elements by the operation $*$ is itself an element of the group.

(2) *Associativity*: i.e. $(a * b) * c = a * (b * c)$ for any elements a, b, c of the group. The order of performing the operation $*$ in combining more than two elements does not affect the final result.

(3) The existence of an *identity* (or neutral) *element*, I, having the property $I * a = a * I = a$ for every element a in the group.

(4) The existence of a unique *inverse element*, denoted by $\bar{a}$, for every element a such that $a * \bar{a} = I = \bar{a} * a$.

If in addition the group exhibits the commutative property, i.e. $a * b = b * a$ for all elements a, b of the group, the group is referred to as a *commutative group* or *Abelian group*.

Illustrations of groups come from many sides.

From number theory:
Finite arithmetics with any modulus under addition
The integers under addition
The positive rationals under multiplication

From geometry:
Various symmetry groups
The set of isometries and their combinations
Vectors under vector addition

From probability theory:
The permutations of a given set of elements

Experience with the structure of *groups* is likely to lead in two directions. The first of these is to consider more than one operation. This leads in due course to definitions of *rings* and *fields*, but what is probably of more immediate concern, to the basic structure of arithmethic and algebra. This can be summarised in the following laws:

	Addition	Multiplication
Commutative law	$a + b = b + a$	$a \cdot b = b \cdot a$
Associative law	$(a + b) + c =$ $a + (b + c)$	$(a \cdot b) \cdot c = a \cdot (b \cdot c)$
Closure	For all elements a, b we can find a third element x so that	

	$a + x = b$	$a \cdot x = b\,(a \neq 0)$
Identity element	$zero$, 0, i.e.	one, 1, i.e.
	$a + 0 = a = 0 + a$	$a \cdot 1 = a = 1 \cdot a$
Inverse element	$a + (-a) = 0 =$	$a \cdot 1/a = 1 = 1/a \cdot a$
	$(-a) + a$	$(a \neq 0)$
Distributive law		$a \cdot (b + c) = (a \cdot b) + (a \cdot c)$

The second direction leads to the idea of *isomorphism* which is the name given to a correspondence between the elements of two groups in which 'products are preserved'. Here the term *product* is used to denote the result of combining two elements by whatever rule of combination is being employed. A simple illustration is the following:

$\times$ mod 5	1	2	4	3
1	1	2	4	3
2	2	4	3	1
4	4	3	1	2
3	3	1	2	4

$\times$ mod 10	1	3	9	7
1	1	3	9	7
3	3	9	7	1
9	9	7	1	3
7	7	1	3	9

If we make the one-to-one correspondence

$$
\begin{array}{cccc}
1 & 2 & 4 & 3 \\
\updownarrow & \updownarrow & \updownarrow & \updownarrow \\
1 & 3 & 9 & 7
\end{array}
$$

between the two groups, we find that the tables are interchangeable. Results in one situation can then be immediately transferred to the other.

The use of *logarithms* is based on an isomorphism between the set of all real numbers under addition and the set of positive real numbers under multiplication. So we have the situation outlined below:

Positive reals (original numbers)		Real numbers (logarithms)
N	$\Longleftrightarrow$	$\log N$
M	$\Longleftrightarrow$	$\log M$
$\times$	$\Longleftrightarrow$	$+$
$N \times M$	$\Longleftrightarrow$	$\log N + \log M$

In any teaching of logarithms this fundamental correspondence must be made clear. This has often been done in the past without any realisation that the situation is not unique. In fact this is a case of the *modern* relating to and interpreting the *traditional*.

Sets and geometry
When we turn to geometry we see that in the early stages, sets are used in the *classification* of various shapes. So, in the first instance, children abstract the meaning of the word *square* by a consideration of the set all of whose members are squares in contrast to another set in which the members are not square. From this experience they may, in due course, learn to *define* the word *square*.

Certainly initial experience with shapes of various kinds is going to help them see the relation of inclusion; that the set of squares, for example, is a sub-set of the set of rectangles, which in turn is a sub-set of the set of parallelograms, etc. So using the classical definitions we arrive at a diagram like Fig. 10.

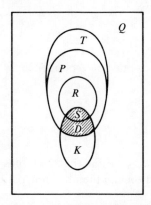

Fig. 10.

$Q = \{$Quadrilaterals$\}$
$T = \{$Trapeziums$\}$
$P = \{$Parallelograms$\}$
$R = \{$Rectangles$\}$
$K = \{$Kites$\}$
$D = \{$Rhombuses (diamonds)$\} = K \cap P$
$S = \{$Squares$\} = D \cap R$

Perhaps a more interesting picture arises if the Venn diagram is drawn in such a way that each of the sets is represented by a closed curve corresponding to the shape of its members, instead of the familiar circle or oval (see Fig. 11).

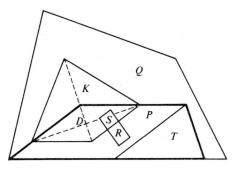

Fig. 11.

An alternative approach is that of dividing quadrilaterals according to the various symmetries they possess. This approach has the merit of leading us quickly to geometrical illustrations of group structures, which can then be compared with groups arising in other connections. The respective *orders* of the different symmetry groups are indicated in Fig. 12.

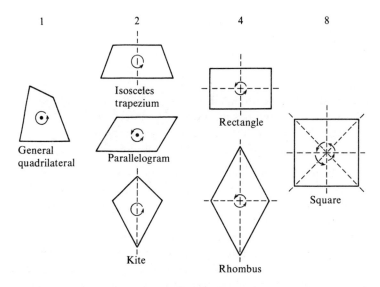

Fig. 12.   Orders of symmetry groups of various quadrilaterals.

A more appropriate Venn diagram is now Fig. 13.

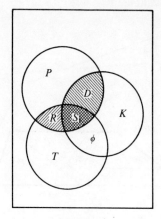

Fig. 13.

T = {Isosceles trapeziums}
　= {Quadrilaterals with line of bilateral symmetry through two sides}
P = {Parallelograms}
　= {Quadrilaterals with half-turn symmetry}
K = {Kites}
　= {Quadrilaterals with line of bilateral symmetry through two vertices}
R = {Rectangles} D = {Rhombuses} S = {Squares}

Note:
T, K, and P all have orders of symmetry, 2
　　$R = P \cap T$ and has an order of symmetry, 4
　　$D = P \cap K$ and has an order of symmetry, 4
　　$S = R \cap D$ and has an order of symmetry, 8

There are *no* quadrilaterals with order of symmetry 4 which includes bilateral symmetry through two sides, and also bilateral symmetry through two vertices, other than the square which has an order of symmetry, 8, i.e. $T \cap K \cap P' = \phi$.

Though classification may form the first part of a modern geometry course, the main part relates to transformation geometry which virtually replaces the Euclidean geometry of traditional courses. Its great advantages mathematically is its links with other branches, with functions, matrix algebra, groups, etc. but most particularly its

28

alliance with algebra. In this way it fits into the overall scheme instead of forming an almost separate area of study with little connection with the other mathematics as is the case with Euclidean geometry. It also has the educational virtue that it lends itself to practical experimentation, with *doing*, rather than listening. Moreover it gives rise in a very natural way to the idea of *congruence*, not only of triangles but figures of any shape. The role of Euclidean geometry as a means of training in *logic* is taken over by a study of mathematical logic in much more general terms. This study itself arises from work on sets, and is considered separately later (see page 35).

Another development which will be followed up by some, mostly those who will take Mathematics further, is a study of vectors. These arise naturally from a consideration of linear displacements, as the intersection, as it were, of a set of displacements all of a given length with a set of displacements all parallel to a given direction.

$\mathcal{E}$ = {Linear displacements}

A = {Displacements of length a}

B = {Displacements in direction $\vec{b}$}

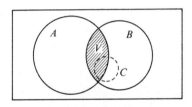

Fig. 14.

So, in Fig. 14, V = {Vectors, $\mathbf{v}$ of length a and direction $\vec{b}$}

If a third set C is defined where C = {Displacements along a given line} where the whole line is in the direction $\vec{b}$, then $V \cap C$ defines the set of *line vectors*, i.e. vectors of length a direction $\vec{b}$, confined to line c. In this case *any* vector along c can be compared with an arbitrary unit vector $\mathbf{c}$ and expressed in the form $k\mathbf{c}$ where k is a scalar taken from the set of real numbers.

The law of vector addition enables us very quickly to define any vector in terms of components along any set of convenient axes (usually at right angles) and thus to be able to characterise a vector by measures along these axes. Thus in Fig. 15, $\mathbf{v} = 4\mathbf{i} + 3\mathbf{j}$, where $\mathbf{i}$

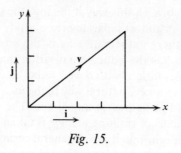

Fig. 15.

and **j** are unit vectors along the x and y axes. If further we use the notation,

$$\mathbf{i} = \begin{pmatrix} 1 \\ 0 \end{pmatrix} \text{and } \mathbf{j} = \begin{pmatrix} 0 \\ 1 \end{pmatrix}$$

we are led naturally to write

$$\mathbf{v} = \begin{pmatrix} 4 \\ 3 \end{pmatrix}$$

and we immediately see another connection between vectors and matrices. The extension to three or more dimensions is immediate.

Sets and relations

Turning from geometry to *relations* we have another oft-recurring theme which deepens and develops throughout the course. A relation between two elements a and b is indicated by an *arrow* from a and b. The elements a and b may be members of the same set, or they may be members of different sets, depending on the nature of the relation. An *equivalence relation* partitions the universal set into a number of equivalence classes. Fig. 16 shows a typical sort of pattern for this situation, and the arrow might for example indicate, 'has the same colour as'.

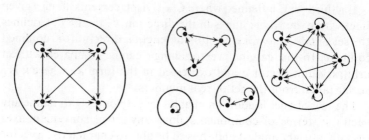

Fig. 16.

It will be noted that a double-headed arrow is used when the relation is symmetric, i.e. when an element a has a certain relation to an element b, and b has the same relation to a. Furthermore, in this particular case, each element has an arrow to itself! This is not true of an ordering relation, such as 'greater than'.

Very often the relation concerns members of elements from different sets. One of the simplest of such relations is the one-to-one correspondence used in defining number. As we progress, the relation may get more and more complicated, and we are led to the idea of 'mapping' one set onto another.

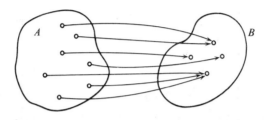

Fig. 17.

Such mappings may be many-to-one as in Fig. 17, many-to-many, one-to-many, or again one-to-one. When all the elements of set A have been used we may find that not all the elements of set B have an arrow to them. This leads us in due course to ideas of domain, range, *onto* and *into* mappings etc. and thus to a precise understanding of *function* which is one of the most fundamental of mathematical concepts. In fact one of the results of using the arrow notation is to release graphs from the *single* Cartesian representation familiar in traditional courses. If we consider, for example, the mapping $f:x \longrightarrow mx$ (or the relation given by $y = mx$) with domain the set of integers, a variety of diagrams can be made. The graphs in Fig. 18 correspond to the case where $m = 2$.

If a number of different values for m are taken, the following general points emerge:

Diagram (a): With two exceptions ($m = 0$, and $m = 1$) two types of picture occur depending on the sign of m, arrows being confined to one side of the diagram for m positive, and crossing over for m negative. It is particularly interesting to note that the picture for $m = a$, and $m = 1/a$ are identical apart from the direction of the arrows.

In the case, $m = 0$ all arrows lead directly to 0; and in the case,

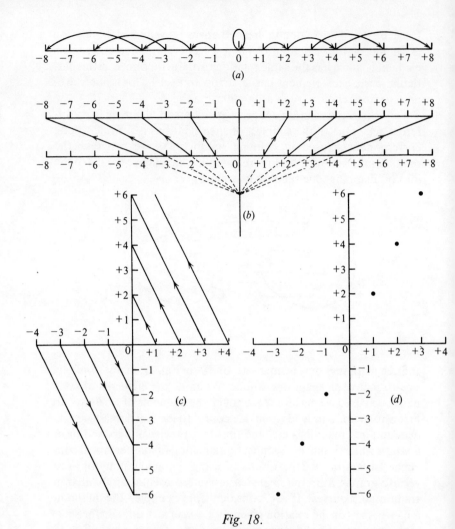

Fig. 18.

$m = 1$, there is a loop back to itself for every point. The special properties of 0 and 1 are thus highlighted very well.

Diagram (*b*): The mapping lines (extended) always pass through a single point except for the value $m = 1$ when the lines are all parallel. Again there is a basic symmetry about the patterns of points corresponding to values of $m = a$, and $m = 1/a$.

Diagram (*c*): The mapping lines in this diagram are always parallel and the 'steepness' of the lines in relation to the axes depends on the value of m. In itself the diagram is not very easy to use, but it represents

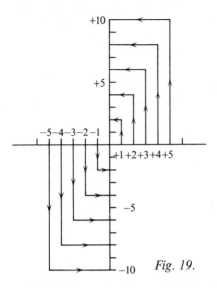

+10

+5

−5−4−3−2−1

+1 +2 +3 +4 +5

−5

−10   *Fig. 19.*

a useful 'half-way house' between diagrams (*b*) and (*d*). The two separate parallel lines of (*b*) have been moved so that their zeros coincide, and are then placed at right angles. The *arrows*, however still connect corresponding points. If these arrows are further modified by drawing them, not straight, but with a 'kink', that is by drawing them so that they run parallel to the new axes, we get the diagram shown in Fig. 19.

The 'kinks' now occur precisely in the same positions as the points (ordered pairs) of diagram (*d*).

Diagram (*d*): This is the traditional cartesian representation, but it can be approached in a slightly different way. If we consider the set of all ordered pairs (x, y) with x and y real, we have the totality of all points in the plane. From this universal set we can consider subsets which obey a certain *rule*, for example y has twice the value of x. When this is done it is found that a 'pattern' emerges, in fact, a straight line through the origin of 'slope 2'.

The continued importance of the traditional representation is that when we move to more complicated 'rules', 'relations', or 'mappings', for example $f:x \longrightarrow x^2$, patterns, though no longer straight lines, can still be recognised. The corresponding pictures for representations (*a*) to (*c*) are not very helpful.

This very brief development indicates how powerful and useful the arrow notation can be in representing relations, but shows also in this case that modern mathematics does not *overthrow* all the

33

traditional, but rather reinforces and adds cogency to, graph work that has long been done in traditional courses.

Sets and statistics

In statistics, certain mappings assume a great importance and chief amongst these is the frequency distribution, one of the fundamental tools of the statistician. This in turn leads to its pictorial representation as a histogram in the case of a finite number of distinct sets, to the frequency polygon and thence to frequency curves. Another strand of statistics is probability and here again work on sets clarifies tremendously ideas such as conditional probability through the idea of the possibility space.

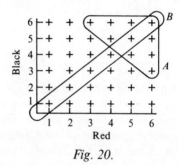

Fig. 20.

In the case of two different sets of 'equally likely' possibilities X and Y, this possibility space is simply the cross-product of sets X and Y or the totality of ordered pairs containing one element of X and one element of Y. Thus, for example, if we have two standard dice (one red, one black) marked with numbers from 1 to 6, and throw them to see what total we get, the possibility space has 36 elements which may be represented by the crosses in Fig. 20. If now I wish to consider the probability of scoring 9 or more with both dice (event A), I can enumerate the possibilities by enclosing them in set A. The probability of event A, written $p(A)$ is clearly $\frac{10}{36}$. If event B is throwing a double, then $p(B) = \frac{6}{36} = \frac{1}{6}$. Now suppose I want to know the probability of *both* A and B occurring, then it is clear that I require the probability of $A \cap B$, which is $\frac{2}{36}$ or $\frac{1}{18}$. On the other hand if I wish to know the probability of getting a double *on the assumption* that my score is 9 or more, this can be seen to be $\frac{2}{10}$ or $\frac{1}{5}$.

Thus $p(A \cap B) = p(A) \cdot p(B \text{ given } A)$
$$\frac{2}{36} = \frac{10}{36} \times \frac{2}{10}$$

Sets and logic
One of the most remarkable things about the theory of sets is that the members of the sets do not themselves have to be *mathematical* entities. It is quite possible for them to have some completely other character. One very important such set is the set of propositions. A proposition is a statement that is either true or false. There can be no other alternative. So in answer to the question, 'Is this proposition true?' we can only reply *yes* or *no*, but not *maybe* or *it depends*.

So a proposition, *p*, has only two states true or false. Its *negation*, *p'* will be false if *p* is true, and true if *p* is false. The same applies to any other proposition, *q*. Two propositions *p* and *q* can be linked by a variety of *connectives* to form further propositions whose truth or falsity depends on the truth or falsity of the propositions *p* and *q*. The simplest of these is the word *and* which will only be true if both *p* and *q* are true. These facts are normally illustrated by means of truth tables. The table for *and* is shown below.

p	*q*	*p and q*
T	T	T
T	F	F
F	T	F
F	F	F

The next most simple connective is the word *or*. In colloquial usage this can sometimes denote either one or the other or both (the *inclusive or*). At other times it can denote either one or the other but *not* both (the *exclusive or*). The difference in the truth tables is seen below:

p	*q*	Inclusive *or*	Exclusive *or*
T	T	T	F
T	F	T	T
F	T	T	T
F	F	F	F

In its mathematical context, each connective is given a *symbol* which uniquely defines the respective truth values of the combined proposition for given truth values of the original statements. Thus for *and*, we use the symbol $\wedge$: for the *inclusive or*, $\vee$; and for the *exclusive or*, $\underline{\vee}$. It is clear that other connectives can be imagined to give all the following possibilities:

p q	1	2 3 4 5	6 7 8 9 10 11	12 13 14 15	16
T T	T	T T T F	T T T F F F	T F F F	F
T F	T	T T F T	T F F T F T	F T F F	F
F T	T	T F T T	F T F T T F	F F T F	F
F F	T	F T T T	F F T F T T	F F F T	F
	t	∨	p q v̲ p' q' ∧		f

Some of these we can recognise already.

Thus Column 2 corresponds to ∨ (inclusive or)
Column 9 corresponds to v̲ (exclusive or)
Column 12 corresponds to ∧ (and)

In addition Column 6 exactly duplicates *p* and is independent of *q*
Column 7 exactly duplicates *q* and is independent of *p*
Column 10 corresponds to the *negation* of *p*, i.e. *p'*
Column 11 corresponds to the *negation* of *q*, i.e. *q'*

If we look at columns 3, 4 and 5 it will be noticed that like column 2 (inclusive or), they contain only one value of F and three of T; and in fact they can be described using *p'* and *q'* with ∨. Thus column 3 corresponds to *p* ∨ *q'*; column 4 to *p'* ∨ *q*; and column 5 to *p'* ∨ *q'*.

In the same way, columns 12, 13, 14, and 15 can all be expressed in terms of ∧. Column 12 corresponds to *p* ∧ *q*; column 13 to *p* ∧ *q'*; column 14 to *p'* ∧ *q*; and column 15 to *p'* ∧ *q'*.

It will be noticed now that column 9 can be expressed as either *p* v̲ *q* or *p'* v̲ *q'*; and that in the same way column 8 is either *p'* v̲ *q* or *p* v̲ *q'*. Put in another way, when statements are combined in these apparently different ways, their resulting truth tables are identical. We then say that the statements are *logically equivalent*.

We are left with the two column 1 and 16. In column 1 we have only T's; in column 16 only F's. We call the first of these a *tautology*, i.e. a proposition that is always true, for example, 'Either it has rained, or it has not.' (*p* or *p'* where *p* stands for 'it has rained'). We call column 16 a *contradiction*, a proposition which is never true. This can be regarded as the negation of a tautology.

One of the commonest connective forms in ordinary English is the form, 'If *p*, then *q*'. The understanding in its ordinary usage is that if *p* is true, then *q* will be true also, and no other conclusions ought to be drawn, in particular in the case when *p* is false. Symbolically it will be found that a single arrow ——→is used for this connective with the extension implied by the following truth table:

$$
\begin{array}{ccc}
p & q & p \longrightarrow q \\
T & T & T \\
T & F & F \\
F & T & T \\
F & F & T \\
\end{array}
$$

For purposes of *logic* we often need to consider the subset of the relation ($\longrightarrow$) where p is true. In this case we use a double arrow $\Longrightarrow$, and write $p \Longrightarrow q$, i.e. whenever p is true, q must also be true if the whole statement is to be true. We then say, 'p implies q'. If in addition 'q implies p' we can use the double-headed arrow, thus $p \Longleftrightarrow q$.

So far we have talked of propositions, or statements that are either true or false. There are many mathematical statements of this form. For example, the statements $2 + 3 = 5, 3 \times 4 = 12, 13 > 9$ are all true; while the statements $3 + 5 = 10, 4 \times 5 = 24, 13 > 16$ are all false. But there are other kinds of statements in mathematics of very great importance. The first of these is the 'open statement', e.g. $x^2 = 25$. In answer to the question, 'Is x^2 equal to 25?' we can only reply, 'Under certain conditions, and depending on the set of numbers we are considering'. If we put $x = 4$, the statement is false; but if we put $x = 5$ then the statement is true. If we are considering the set of integers, then if we put $x = -5$ the statement will again be true. We say then that the values 5 and -5 form the solution or truth set of the open statement, $x^2 = 25$.

In terms of implication, if p is the statement '$x = 5$' and q the statement '$x^2 = 25$', then it is fair to write $p \Longrightarrow q$, as whenever p is true, q is true. On the other hand if we are considering the set of real numbers, we cannot write $q \Longrightarrow p$, as it is not necessarily the case that when q is true that p is true, since p could be -5. Many of the difficulties of elementary algebra are avoided if the symbols $\Longrightarrow$ and $\Longleftarrow$ are properly used instead of the more conventional sign for therefore $\therefore$, which was used for both kinds of situation.

Another kind of statement is that of the formula, which expresses a true relationship between two or more quantities, e.g. $C = \pi d$. Here if numerical values are given to either C or d, the statement becomes an open statement which will give rise to a proper truth set for the other.

This basic work in logic can be extended in various directions, to the combination of more than two statements into the whole realm of propositional logic, or to comparisons with circuit theory and thus to Boolean algebra and the basic elements of a computer. But whereas elementary logic is something that we need to teach all students, the further applications will probably be restricted to the more able and those likely to continue with Mathematics as a main subject of study.

Flow charts and computers

If work on sets represents the most radical strand of modern mathematics, there are others which also play an important role. One is the acknowledgement of the fact that the electronic computer has come to stay and that its existence is going to alter not only our whole way of life but also our whole way of thinking. Problems which previously were considered insoluble because of the sheer time involved in mechanical manipulation can now be dealt with by the computer because of its immense speed of computation, provided only that the *steps* it has to follow are correctly and logically laid out. This is done in the first instance by means of a *flow chart*.

A flow chart consists of a series of steps indicated by boxes separated by arrows which show the direction in which the process is to continue. Some of these boxes contain simple instructions, e.g.: 'Add 10', 'Transfer the answer to store X', 'Bring the contents of store Y to the accumulator', etc. These are usually enclosed in a rectangle. Others are decision boxes which offer alternative routes according to whether the answer is *yes* or *no*, e.g.: 'Is the answer greater than 10?' 'Is $X = Y$?' Decision boxes are usually rhombuses or elongated hexagons. The arrows from a decision box may progress to another part of the program, or they may go back to an earlier stage so that the process is repeated in a modified form. This

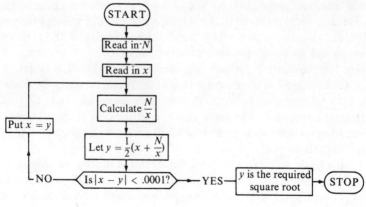

Fig. 21.

is called a loop. A simple flow chart is shown (Fig. 21) for finding the square root of a number N when the first estimate of the square root is x. Note that a given degree of precision is assumed here, namely that the two estimates of the square root should not differ by more than .0001. A greater degree of precision could be obtained if required. In the previous example, a flow chart is used to solve a problem. It can also be used to define a process (see Fig. 22).

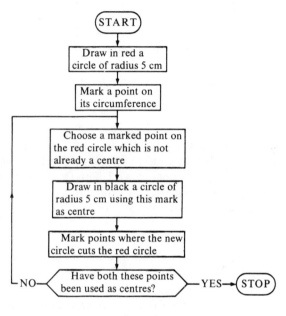

Fig. 22.

Flow charts then indicate a way of thinking that *can* be translated for use by computers but which have value in themselves, and so are used in many places in different forms. If one can write a foolproof flow chart to represent a process, then it is certain that the process is understood! So flow charts will appear in the mathematics of all students. For some there will be a study of computers themselves in varying degrees of depth – the idea of binary numbers, the use of calculating machines, circuit theory; *and, or* and other gates; and if they are fortunate enough to have access to a machine, the translation of flow charts into programs by means of a suitable *language* so that the programs are actually run. But everyone should come across flow charts.

Besides the use of flow charts, one other aspect of the influence of computing on mathematical thinking should be mentioned and that is a new emphasis on *iterative* processes, i.e. repeated looping, and on *approximation* – but to any degree of accuracy required. Numbers in computers belong to the *set of rationals*, and do *not* include the theoretical mathematical concepts implied by radicals and by numbers like π which are not rational. Thus whereas the number π represents a mathematical concept which is theoretically *exact*, $\pi = C/d$, in any practical situation and in any calculation by computer we have to give a value to π which is *not exact*, but sufficiently accurate for the purposes we have in mind. This, in turn, means that we must train students to consider the degree of accuracy which is appropriate, bearing in mind the accuracy of measurements made, or the decisions which are to be made as a result of the calculation. Another possible source of difficulty is in the reversibility of certain statements. For example, it is mathematically correct to say that for positive x, $x^2 = 2 \Longleftrightarrow x = \sqrt{2}$. However, if $\sqrt{2}$ is calculated it will never be exact. If we take the common value of 1.414, then when this is squared the result is 1.999396 which is certainly very close to 2, but not *exactly* 2. This theoretical loss, however, is as nothing compared with the prodigious accuracy and speed with which calculations can now be carried out by computer.

Modern approaches to problem solving
Another significant strand to modern mathematics is the approach to problem solving. More often than not in the past the only problems that children met in mathematics were those set in exercises by the teachers to which the solution was *already known*, and for the solution of which exactly the right amount of information was given and a definite process or method expected. From the point of view of 'transfer' to real life situations this experience was often fairly useless. Problems in real life are frequently incoherently stated in the first case. The information available is often insufficient, or at the other extreme, too detailed, and the method of approach is *not* predetermined. In fact many different approaches may yield solutions. So there is an attempt to incorporate into mathematics lessons 'the investigation' where the student's own inventiveness and creativity is called into play, where the student must decide how to proceed and often create his own symbolism in order to reach a conclusion. In all this he is *doing* mathematics at a level at which he is competent.

If we examine the steps through which we go in the solution of a problem we may be able to see a fairly consistent pattern. Professor

Fig. 23.

Polya in his book, *How to Solve It* lists four steps as in the flow chart in Fig. 23.

The first, often the hardest, and yet most fundamental step is either understanding the problem (if it is given you by someone else), or framing it in such a way that it is tractable to mathematical techniques. This is the stage of forming a 'mathematical model', of defining terms, of rejecting extraneous information and concentrating on certain basic essentials, of clarifying the implications of what we are trying to do. This clarification may well lead to some free experimentation, a basic trial and error method with simple values during which we constantly search for a pattern, for relationships between elements, for similarities with previous problems so that we can devise a suitable plan of attack. Once the plan is formulated we can fall back on all the mathematical techniques we have learned and the skills we have acquired in order to carry out the plan. We may, of course, not have sufficient skills, in which case there is a *real growing point* as there will be a genuine motivation to acquire them. This may involve seeking help from others and/or reference to books on related topics. Our carrying out of the plan involves us in recording and in explaining our procedure until a solution is obtained. Having done this we look back to see whether the problem is completely solved, or whether, with adaptations there are further generalisations or applications or implications possible. It may happen that we shall be able to *prove* that *no solution* is possible – see the Königsberg Bridge problem (p. 17) – in which case this constitutes the culmination of the problem.

Measurement

In developing these strands of modern mathematics it is important not to lose sight of significant strands in traditional course work. One of the chief of these is the application of mathematics to everyday life, and foremost amongst these applications is the whole process of measurement. Any process of measurement involves the following procedure (see Fig. 24):

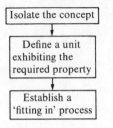

Fig. 24.

The first thing to do is to isolate the concept from all the extraneous features with which it is associated. So for example, every solid object has properties of length, area, volume, weight (mass) and density, and usually it is only *one* of these that we are concerned with at any given moment.

We next choose some object displaying the property concerned and *arbitrarily* assign this as the *unit* of measure. For social convenience it is important that as wide a body of people as possible should agree on this unit but *mathematically* any unit is satisfactory. We then require a process whereby this unit can either be reproduced or we can establish a *ratio* between the property of the object with which we are concerned and the same property displayed by the unit. So

$$\textit{Measure (of length)} = \frac{\text{Length of object}}{\text{Length of unit}}$$

[where length can be replaced by area, volume, mass, etc.]

It often happens that this cannot be done directly, but that we have to rely on certain properties of matter so that this ratio is in fact established by means of a *proportion*. Thus for example, one device for *weighing* is dependent on the idea that the weight of an object is proportional to the extension it causes in a spring. We then say,

$$\begin{aligned}\text{Measure of weight} &= \frac{\text{Weight of object}}{\text{Weight of unit}} \\ &= \frac{\text{Extension of spring by object}}{\text{Extension of spring by unit}}\end{aligned}$$

and it is, in fact, the extensions that are measured, *not* the weights.

42

The same principle applies very much to thermometers where the temperature is defined in terms of the *comparative expansion* caused in various materials such as mercury, or gas, etc. Likewise electrical measurements are made by comparisons of deflections within a galvanometer.

Two points need to be stressed. The first is that the use of the equals sign in this case really means 'equal as accurately as the measuring instrument will allow'. Thus it *can* happen with inaccurate instruments that the relationship *equals* is *not transitive*. Thus if *A* is weighed equal to *B*, and *B* to *C* and *C* to *D*, it may happen that a direct comparison of *A* with *D* would not produce equality! This often happens with classroom rulers where there may be appreciable differences in measures of say a metre. Thus in every measurement there is a degree of error dependent on instrument and user, and we cannot really speak of *exactitude*, but only of measurements to within a given *margin of error*. Consider, for example, measuring a pencil. This process can be carried through in successive stages by reference to Fig. 25. The pencil is longer than 6 cm but shorter than 7. However, its length is nearer to 7 cm than to 6 cm so we say, 'It is 7 cm long *to the nearest centimetre*' (*a*).

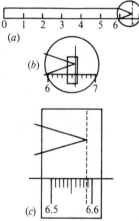

Fig. 25.

When we use tenths of a centimetre or millimetres, (*b*) we find that the length of the pencil now comes between 6.5 cm and 6.6 cm but is nearer to 6.6 cm. We say that it is 6.6 cm *to the nearest tenth of a centimetre* or *to the nearest millimetre*.

If we could imagine a further enlargement (*c*), we could see that to the nearest $\frac{1}{100}$ cm the length would be 6.59 cm though even this is not

43

the *exact* length of the pencil. We have, however, successively reduced our margin of error, from one centimetre in case (*a*) to a tenth of a centimetre in case (*b*) and to a hundredth of a centimetre in case (*c*).

In situations other than in the science laboratory we rarely look for a degree of accuracy greater than 'to the nearest millimetre'. But such accuracy is better stated as a relative error, rather than an absolute one. To make this clear suppose you were asked to mark off intervals of 10 cm and that you were consistently 1 mm short. This means that you actually measure 99 mm instead of 100 mm, an error of 1%. This may seem unimportant, but if you did this ten times, your measure of a metre would be 1 cm short. If you now used this measure of a metre to lay out a 100 metre race track, you would finish up a whole metre short. This is still only a 1% error, but it may no longer seem unimportant! So accuracy, margins of error, significant figures are concepts which must always be kept in mind in any practical situation.

The second point is that all measurements made by instrument, by definition, are *ratios* and therefore correspond to the set of positive rationals. It is this that makes the idea of *surds* and other non-rational real numbers so hard, for here we are idealising in the number system by requiring measures which are both *exact* and *non-rational*!

Drawing three dimensional objects
A second major strand within the 'utilitarian objectives' of mathematics is the attempt to represent three dimensional objects from everyday life on a flat piece of paper, a two dimensional space. These representations are many and various and are used according to the

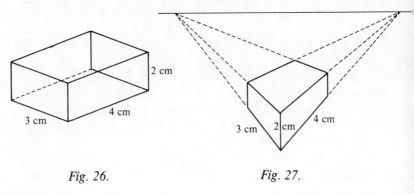

Fig. 26.   *Fig. 27.*

requirements of the situation. To illustrate this point, let us consider a variety of representations of a cuboid of dimensions 2 cm by 3 cm by 4 cm. This may be drawn 'in general position' without attempting to portray the dimensions accurately, but acknowledging certain features, viz. that the edges are parallel in fours (Fig. 26).

It may occur that a figure drawn in this way, particularly if it is large, 'doesn't look right' and we then resort to the device of the artists of the realistic school by introducing a horizon and vanishing points (Fig. 27). This is the physical representation of the statement, 'Parallel lines meet at infinity.'

We may try to introduce realism by accurately portraying as much as possible. So we can get oblique projection, in which one face is accurately portrayed, but the other lengths and angles are inaccurate (Fig. 28). This is a useful device for *prisms* where the cross-section can be shown accurately.

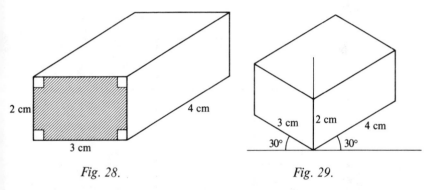

Fig. 28.   Fig. 29.

Or we may be concerned with actual measurements in three dimensions at right angles in which case we use *isometric* projection (Fig. 29). In this case *no* angles are correctly shown, but using the correct instruments good drawings can be made quickly, and neatly, and the visual impression is good.

We may try to develop the views from three aspects accurately as in *plans and elevations*. Two main developments are shown in Fig. 30, known as first and third angle projections. In either of these approaches we have, as it were, dissected the solid!

We may be concerned with constructing the solid, in which case we produce a *net* (Fig. 31).

In every case it is seen that the representation involves some measure of *distortion* but this is inevitable. What is of importance is how to minimise this distortion in relation to our immediate objec-

45

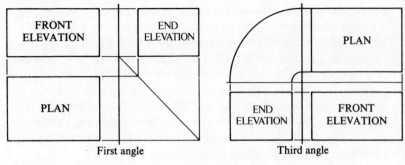

| FRONT ELEVATION | END ELEVATION |
| PLAN | |

First angle

| | PLAN |
| END ELEVATION | FRONT ELEVATION |

Third angle

Fig. 30.

tives. It is of interest to try to make a three-dimensional representation of a four-dimensional 'cuboid' where again some distortion is inevitable, but the very attempt makes clear the fundamental difficulty.

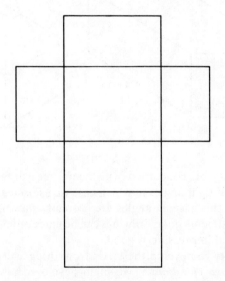

Fig. 31.

The triangle

A third strand which appears to many to be something of an obsession is the prominence given in geometry to the study of the triangle. Thus much of Euclidean geometry is dependent on the congruence of triangles. Clearly congruence is a concept which has applications

46

to figures of all shapes, both plane and solid, and yet many people used to leave school believing that the only things that could be congruent were triangles! Whereas this is obviously absurd, there are good practical reasons for still giving considerable emphasis to the triangle. The first is that every polygon can be divided into triangles, so that when we study triangles we have a basic framework for our study of all polygons. The second is that triangles are the only rigid polygonal shape. Make any other polygon out of rods (strips of cardboard or *Meccano*) and joints (paper clips) and it will flop around. Put in some diagonals to divide the polygon into triangles and it is at once firm. It is for this reason that steel frameworks are usually built up of triangles, and that doors and gates are often 'braced' by putting a diagonal piece across them.

Because of these two properties, 'triangulation' is the basis of much survey work. It is also used in astronomy to calculate the distance away of the stars. Of course for these applications, another notion, that of *similarity* in a traditional course (enlargement in a modern course) is necessary. This involves the idea of constant ratio between corresponding lengths (i.e. scale) and that of congruence of corresponding angles.

The starting point in all this, of course, is the right angled triangle for a number of reasons:

(1) Every other triangle can be shown to be either the sum or difference of two right triangles (see Fig. 32).

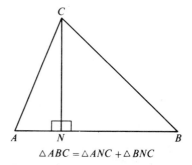
$\triangle ABC = \triangle ANC + \triangle BNC$

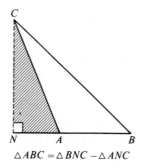
$\triangle ABC = \triangle BNC - \triangle ANC$

Fig. 32.

(2) Since one angle is already known to be 90° and the angle sum of a triangle is 180°, if we know *one* other angle, the *shape* of the triangle is fixed, and the proportions of all the sides are determined.

47

(3) The lengths of the three sides of a right angled triangle are connected by the relationship known as Pythagoras' Theorem.

The second result quoted above can give rise to solutions at two distinct levels, (*a*) the drawing of *scale* figures, which is fairly elementary, and (*b*) the use of the trigonometrical ratios, sine, cosine, and tangent. The difference is one of accuracy and sophistication. But both use the same basic principle.

The circle and sphere

If the triangle is one fundamental block of mensuration, the circle is another. Very early on, students should know the fundamental relationship of the circumference and diameter of the circle, $C = \pi d$. This is a relation of linear measures. When we come to consider the *area* of a circle, we can build on our work on triangles by thinking of the circle as the limiting form of a regular polygon of *n* sides, each of length *b*. So in Fig. 33,

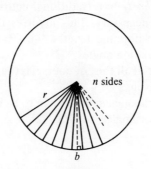

Fig. 33.

Area of each triangle $= \frac{1}{2}rb$
Area of all triangles $= n\,(\frac{1}{2}rb)$
$\qquad\qquad\qquad\quad = \frac{1}{2}r(nb)$
But *nb* is approximately equal to *C*
So Area of circle $= \frac{1}{2}rC$
Substituting the value, $C = 2\pi r$ we get
Area of circle $= \frac{1}{2}r(2\pi r) = \pi r^2$

This approach has two great virtues: (i) it anticipates the later approach of the calculus, and (ii) with slight adaptation it yields the formula for the area of a *sector* of a circle in terms of radius *r* and length of arc, *L* (Fig. 34):
Area of Sector $= \frac{1}{2}rL$
This in turn can be adapted to find the surface area of a cone.

48

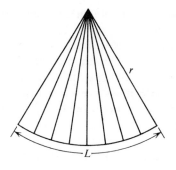

Fig. 34.

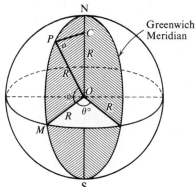

Fig. 35.

In the previous section much was said of the applications of the study of the triangle to practical situations in two and three dimensions where the figure of study can be broken up into one or more plane triangles. But of course, any large scale map-making has got to face up to the problem that the surface of the earth is not plane, but curved and indeed for most practical purposes can be thought of as the surface of a sphere. Just as it is possible to locate the position of a point on a plane by reference to two co-ordinates – conventionally (x, y) or (r, θ) – so on the surface of the earth we can fix the position of a point by two co-ordinates, its longitude and its latitude. This idea should, I think, be understood by all secondary school leavers.

The earth is considered to be divided by a number of meridian planes all intersecting along the N–S axis, and one of these, the plane of the Greenwich meridian is taken as the reference meridian and is labelled $0°$ (Fig. 35). Any other meridian plane forms an angle θ with this plane, and this angle is called the angle of *longitude*, either East or West.

49

Having located the meridian on which a point lies, we have now the comparatively simple job of locating a point on a line. We first consider the plane of the equator which goes through the centre of the earth and is normal to the N – S axis. This cuts the meridian plane in a line OM whose length is R, the radius of the earth. The point M is the starting point or zero marker for latitude. We now use the idea that lengths North or South of M, are proportional to the angle subtended at the centre, i.e. $PM \propto \phi$. This angle ϕ is termed the *latitude* North or South of the equator. It happens that the locus of all points P with latitude ϕ is a circle whose plane is parallel to that of the equator, and whose radius CP is equal to $R \cos \phi$.

It is perhaps of interest to note that finding one's latitude has always been a simpler thing to do than finding one's longitude. The reason for this is that when the sun is directly above a point M on the equator, its rays form an angle ϕ with the vertical (OP continued) at any point P on the same meridian (see Fig. 36). On the other hand to determine one's longitude, one needs an accurate way to measure time so as to be able to find the time elapsed between the instants at which the sun is overhead on the Greenwich meridian, and when it is overhead on the meridian where one happens to be.

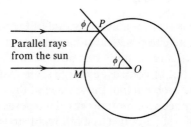

Fig. 36.

Methods of calculation

If measurement is one of the prime applications of mathematics to everyday life, it would be virtually useless without methods of calculation that bring the operations that have to be performed within reasonable bounds. Of course it is an essential pre-condition that children entering secondary school should know their number bonds both for addition and subtraction, and for multiplication and division. If this is not the case on entry, then it will have to form an important part of any programme of teaching until it is.

But even when one knows one's tables well, and can deal properly with the fixing of the decimal point in any calculation, any practical (i.e. real) problem is likely to involve one in heavy calculation which is fearfully time consuming and not very mathematically productive. It was to meet precisely this point that logarithms were introduced historically, and they are still necessary today for much the same reason. There are, however, today other aids to calculation which in many places are superseding the use of logarithms, such as the slide rule, the hand calculating machines, and of course computers.

The slide rule is the least expensive and has the merit of being easily portable. It is an essential tool in engineering and useful in a number of other professions. It is easy and quick to use and gives much the same degree of accuracy as four-figure logarithms. The effective use of the slide rule depends on two subordinate skills which are useful in themselves:

(1) The ability to approximate, or get a realistic estimate of size, and

(2) The ability to read scales to successive degrees of accuracy, fixing up to four significant figures though three is the common limit. Moreover a real understanding of the slide rule rests upon an understanding of logarithms though it is, of course, possible to set out procedures which work and give no insight. So to multiply M by N, consider the flow chart in Fig. 37. For some this skill itself will suffice. For others the underlying theory will be regarded not only as of interest, but of vital importance.

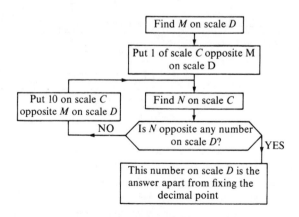

Fig. 37.

Hand calculating machines are likewise finding an increasing place in the facilities of some schools in various parts of the world. They are particularly useful in generating an understanding of place value, and of the truth of the commutative, associative, and distributive laws as applied to the processes of addition and multiplication.

Once the processes to carry out the various operations have been mastered, the complexity of the numbers is comparatively unimportant and again the mind is released to do positive mathematical thinking instead of being bogged down in figures. So we find the use of calculating machines gives rise to a whole new set of procedures including iterative processes which one can carry out reasonably quickly but which hitherto have been unthinkable because of the time taken.

These points lead to the next – the value of the machines as an introduction to computers. A conventional machine has three registers, the setting register, the accumulator and the cycle. Consider now a simple program for adding two numbers, say X and Y (Fig. 38). We have here all the ingredients of a computer program – the *data* (X and Y), the *input* or *read* statements (Put X in setting register), the program which defines the order of operations, and the *output* or *print* statements (write down the number in accumulator).

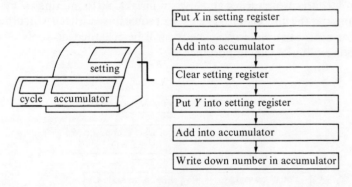

Fig. 38.

Valuable as both slide rule and hand calculating machines can be, however, in many parts of the world they will be beyond the bounds of financial possibility whereas tables of logarithms will not. Moreover such tables contain a great deal more information such as tables of squares, square roots, reciprocals, trigonometric functions and so on. So they will remain a necessary and valuable aid to computation.

Some final remarks in this section need to be made. Whatever aids to computation are used, there are a number of principles that always apply:

(1) Checks should always be made to ensure freedom from absurd blunders.

(2) Careful consideration must be given to the precision with which a problem is stated and the degree of accuracy of the suggested solution.

(3) Alternative methods should be considered in advance, and the most suitable chosen.

Basic algebra

Mention was made earlier of the modern terminology of open sentences and truth sets to work that has traditionally been described as 'solving equations'. The point is that whatever description is used, work of this kind should be included in the mathematical education of all students.

The basic idea is that of using a letter to stand for an unknown quantity. In its basic form the unknown is a number. Later it may stand for something more complicated, a vector or a matrix. In problem solving, the letter is used in a sentence, or sentences to describe its properties in relation to other quantities – equations are formed. We then have a series of techniques which are used to simplify the equation until a solution, or solution set is found. To do this, certain understandings are necessary:

(1) Any number can be described in many ways.

(2) In an equation when we say that two sides are equal, we are really using two different descriptions of the same thing. The emphasis in this approach is on each side, and maintaining equality.

(3) So whatever we do to one side we must do to the other; otherwise the descriptions would no longer be equivalent.

(4) If $A = B$, then A can be subtituted for B and B can be substituted for A in any other equation because again A and B are two different ways of describing the same number, and whatever is true of one description will be true of the other.

(5) In the same way, two or more equations may be added, or subtracted or multiplied by the same number.

(6) Likewise we can usually divide both sides by the same number, but there is one exception. We can not divide by *zero*.

(7) This is a particular example of some steps being reversible and others not. So:

$$a \cdot 0 = 0$$
$$b \cdot 0 = 0 \implies a \cdot 0 = b \cdot 0$$

but this does *not* imply that $a = b$.

[This traditional approach should be contrasted with the 'modern' one where the emphasis is on the *full statement* and the equivalence of that *statement* with each succeeding one. Contrast the 'explanation' of the following sequence by the two methods:

$$3x - 5 = 4 \quad (1)$$
$$3x = 9 \quad (2)$$
$$x = 3$$

In both cases to line (1) we 'add 5 to both sides'; and on line (2) 'divide both sides by three'. It should be noted that the *names* or *descriptions* of the successive numbers on the right hand side (and therefore on the left) are 4, 9 and 3, that is they repeatedly change. With 'modern terminology' the successive *statements* are *equivalent*, that is they all have the same truth sets, namely {3}.]

Letters can also be used, however, to describe general relations and these are generally referred to as formulae. Formulae can be rearranged by the same rules as those mentioned above, and frequently this is useful if it enables us to so rearrange a formula that the one quantity whose value we seek exists by itself on one side of the formula. It is then said to be the 'subject of the formula'. This is natural as it is its simplest name. The other name is more complicated but possibly for the moment more useful!

Graph work

Graph work, using Cartesian axes, has long been regarded as the meeting point of algebra and geometry and thus central to the development of mathematics in the secondary school. Although modern mathematics does suggest alternative ways of representing graphs (see p. 32) it is clear that conventional graph work must still occupy a central position. The terminology may be somewhat different, the essential skills remain the same. Thus where traditionally we would say, 'Draw the graph of $y = x^2$', in modern terminology we would say, 'Represent the mapping $f: x \longrightarrow x^2$'

At the secondary school level the *idea* of being able to make mappings (draw graphs) of complicated relations is fundamental. So also is the idea that if two such mappings (graphs) are drawn on the same axes, the intersection of the two graphs represents the *solution* to a pair of simultaneous equations.

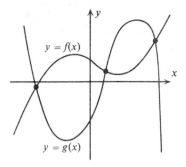

$y = f(x)$

$y = g(x)$

Fig. 39.

Thus as a *general method* of solving a pair of simultaneous equations, $y = f(x)$ and $y = g(x)$, we can draw the graph of the two functions and find their point(s) of intersection (Fig. 39). It may be that this is not very accurate, but should we require greater accuracy we can enlarge the regions near the points of intersection.

The method can be extended very powerfully to solve equations in one variable, x, of considerable complexity. Thus a solution to an equation like $x^2 = \sin x$ can be obtained by introducing a variable y, drawing graphs of the now simultaneous equations $y = x^2$ and $y = \sin x$ and finding where they intersect. At the level we are concerned with an interesting application is the solution of all *quadratic* equations by the use of graph $y = x^2$, and the graph of some appropriate

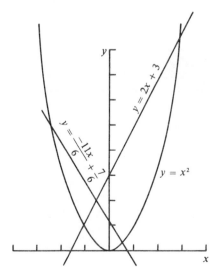

$y = 2x + 3$

$y = -\frac{11x}{6} + \frac{7}{6}$

$y = x^2$

Fig. 40.

55

linear equation. In the simple case $x^2 = 2x + 3$, it is clear that we can draw the graphs of $y = x^2$ and $y = 2x + 3$.

In the more complicated case, $6x^2 + 11x - 7 = 0$, we first re-organise the equation to $6x^2 = -11x + 7$ and then

$$x^2 = \frac{-11x}{6} + \frac{7}{6}$$

and now draw the graphs of $y = x^2$ and

$$y = \frac{-11x}{6} + \frac{7}{6}$$

This brings us back to our dependence on a thorough understanding of familiarity with the linear equation, and its graphical representation as a straight line graph. In its simplest form it passes through the origin. When this occurs it can be regarded simply as a 'multiplier' line, or a conversion line, or the set of all points who co-ordinates x and y bear the simple relation, $y/x = $ constant, say k. In particular if k itself is a fraction, integer values of y and x give rise to the set of all simple fractions equivalent to k (Fig. 41). In the slightly more general form $y = mx + c$, we can either regard the line as displaced in the y-direction a distance c, giving an intercept on the y-axis of c, or alternatively, by rewriting the equation in the form $y = m(x + c/m)$ and substituting $Y = y$, $X = x + c/m$ we convert the equation to $Y = mX$ where there is now a change of origin along the x-axis a distance $-c/m$.

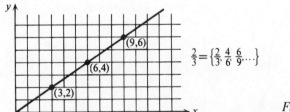

$$\frac{2}{3} = \left\{ \frac{2}{3}, \frac{4}{6}, \frac{6}{9}, \ldots \right\}$$

Fig. 41.

The straight line graph is so easy to comprehend, so powerful to use that it is frequently used in scientific work. The experimenter tries to establish a correspondence between two sets of quantities by assuming that readings, but for experimental error, would lie on a straight line, which he calls the 'line of best fit'. If this doesn't work, he resorts to using logarithms and tries to establish a linear relation between logarithms.

The fact that the gradient of a straight line is a measure of 'average rate of change' together with the idea of successively smaller intervals and of a limit, leads us into the elements of the differential calculus and the idea of the derivative of a function. This is important in so many applications that it seems to me it could be argued that in any technological society, it is one of the concepts required as a 'utilitarian objective' for the vast majority.

Euclidean geometry
With so much new material included in the course, something has got to suffer, and it appears that the most likely candidate is Euclidean Geometry mostly because its development is so isolated from the main stream of the course. However in its development in the past there have been traditionally three stages, *A, B*, and *C*.

Stage A is the experimental stage, the stage of learning terms and definitions, coming to grips with ideas of points, lines, planes, angles, and so on and some of the figures, plane and solid, which are made up of these components. The fundamental criteria necessary for the construction of a triangle would fall into this category. This work, of course, is still essential, but as has been said above, work on sets can interpret much that is done at this stage. Moreover by its emphasis on symmetry it can bring many insights which were previously implicit but not stressed.

Stage B was the stage at which deductions were made from certain results that were assumed. This was the start in the development of the learning of logic, and some work of this kind is still desirable though again the *logic* may be applied to situations which are non-Euclidean as well as Euclidean. So we expect to develop results like the following:

The angle sum of a triangle is 180°.

The angle sum of a polygon of n sides is $(2n - 4)$ right angles.

The line joining the midpoints of two sides of a triangle is parallel to the third side and equal in length to half of it.

The first of these results will probably now come from a study of tessellations; but its extension to polygons of n sides is still appropriate. The second result will also be recognisable from tessellations and will become further apparent when we come to consider translations and rotations. The shaded triangles in Fig. 42 are related to each other by translation.

Any shaded triangle can take up the position of an unshaded triangle by rotation about the midpoint of a side, or about a vertex.

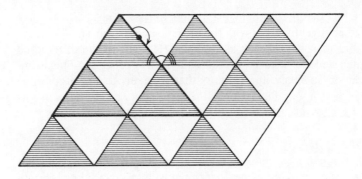

Fig. 42.

Similarly the theorems of parallel lines and various properties of parallelograms emerge from the same work. The point is that certain of the *results* are important in their own right and that these results arise from a *process of rational deduction*. These are the two essential ingredients, but the premises from which these deductions are made can be either traditional or modern.

Stage C was the building up of a complete logical structure from certain axioms, these axioms being the ones proposed by Euclid. It is this stage that can now legitimately be dropped. This is because the basic elements required in building up such a structure can more easily be seen in many other situations, both algebraic and geometric. Moreover the structures thus developed are not so monolithic in character. They can be more easily encompassed and compared, and in this way the essential features can be appreciated. Once again the *value* of building up such structures is not denied. It represents, indeed, one of the cultural appreciations mentioned in the previous chapter.

Summary of content
The themes outlined above constitute some of the important threads that permeate many courses of mathematics in secondary schools. In addition if approached in a proper way, they offer the possibility of achieving the aims suggested in the previous chapter, those of utility, cultural background, aesthetic appreciation, enjoyment, personal development and fulfilment. Moreover they can be fitted into an overall *scheme* so that the different parts of the course supplement and reinforce learning. They are summarised in Fig. 43.

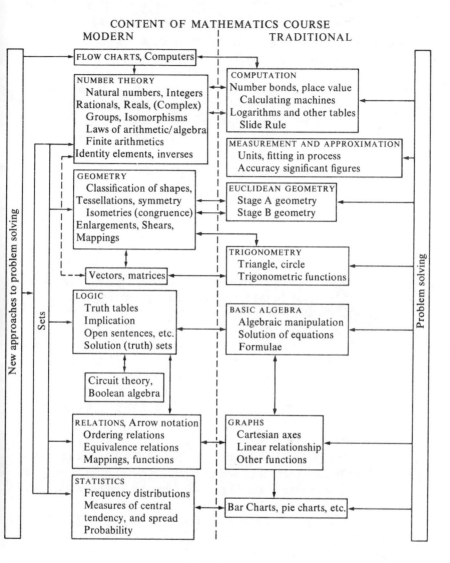

Fig. 43.

The most important features of this diagram are the following:

(1) Modern and Traditional features of the course inter-relate and are complementary at every stage. There is no question of modern mathematics replacing or overthrowing the traditional.

Rather it interprets, and possibly offers new understandings, strategies, and approaches, and incorporates some of the more recent developments in mathematics.

(2) 'Problems' and 'New Approaches to Problem Solving' impinge upon and relate to everything in the course. Mathematics is concerned with the posing of problems, the expression of these in precise mathematical language or symbolism, the searching for patterns in their solution, the development of necessary skills for the same purpose, and then with establishing that the methods used satisfy the highest criteria of logical inference.

(3) Sets permeate practically every topic.

The content outlined above is seen to be the *core* of most mathematics courses at the secondary school level. There will, of course, have to be modifications according to the students we are teaching, their abilities and aspirations. For the less able not *all* the material should be included. On the other hand for the more able the course should not be limited to what has been outlined. Rather the framework offered here should form a springboard for mathematical progress in a variety of directions.

We come now to consider the *organisation* of the content into a usable form for the teacher. The chief points for our consideration are the nature of the material itself and the developing nature and psychological needs of the pupils who come under our care.

If we take the second point first, students on arrival will come from a variety of schools and will have been taught by a variety of teachers using a wide variety of methods and with very different ideas of standards and appropriate achievement. Our job is to mould these into a reasonably coherent whole, to discover weaknesses and omissions in previous teaching, and yet while trying to remedy these, to do so in such a way that it is not psychologically damaging. We also want to instil a sense of newness, of purpose, and of difference from previous schools so that the transition to secondary school really does represent an advance. We want to make sure that basic work in number and measurement is really understood but *not* at the expense of tedious revision which will kill any responsiveness to the new situation in which the students find themselves.

Possible starting points are thus sets themselves, using a comparatively advanced symbolism which is unlikely to have been taught in Primary Schools; or to discuss number representation in different bases which stresses place value, and involves students in a great deal of practice with tables(!); to begin with mathematical series, and their patterns; or to consider three dimensional objects and the inter-relationship of faces, vertices and edges, and of concepts of length, area, volume and weight.

The next thing that we want to ensure is a sort of spiral development, or cyclic rotation of topics so that we return at intervals to the same topic or theme and develop it further. This ensures that no topic or theme is ever very far removed from the forefront of our attention and thus forgotten, and that there is a definite gradation in difficulty. However, it will still be necessary to incorporate regular periods of revision which should occur more frequently than just the end of term or end of year!

As the students come towards the end of their course we must ensure that we fully bear in mind their hopes and aspirations. If this involves the passing of some particular examination we *must* spend time in preparation and practice for this great hurdle, setting practice tests of the same style and difficulty as the event itself, so that when it comes, it is not so traumatic or unusual, but can be taken in one's stride. If no such examination is required, then we must look to the applications in the kind of life that our students are likely to live after they leave school.

When we come to the material itself we find that *within* any one topic there is usually a fairly natural order in which later developments are dependent on prior understandings. However, progression from one topic to another in terms of the overall syllabus is not so straightforward for frequently it appears that several items ought to be developed as it were in parallel. So it may be that topics, A, B, and C have to be covered before we progress to D (Fig. 44). However the classroom situation requires us to arrange the work in a *series* of consecutive lessons. In these circumstances it is up to a point an arbitrary decision as to which of A, B, or C should be taught first. Considerations of this kind lead us again to resort to a spiral development in which aspects of *Number and Number Theory*, *Shape and Measurement*, and *Relations and Graphs* are kept more or less going

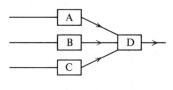

Fig. 44.

in rotation. These categorisations are somewhat arbitrary and certain topics may seem to belong under one or more headings but it is nevertheless helpful to use such nomenclature in trying to analyse a course.

It may be instructive to see just how this works with two courses of very different origin, and thought of originally in connection with pupils of very different ability. The first of these is the *School Mathematics Project* which is now widely known both in England and abroad, and was originally designed for pupils of above average ability though the present courses now cover most of the ability range. We will denote the various sections by letters as follows:

Number and Number Theory	A
Shape and Measurement	B
Relations and Graphs	C
Revision	R

Then the breakdown of the SMP course by chapters (as far as can be done by single letters) is outlined below:

BOOK 1

	A	B	C	R
1. A New Look at Arithmetic	A			
2. Sets	A			
3. Co-ordinates			C	
4. Fractions	A			
Revision Exercises				R
5. Angle		B		
6. Number Patterns	A			
7. Sequences and Relations			C	
8. Polygons and Polyhedra		B		
Revision Exercises				R
9. Decimal Fractions	A			
10. Area		B		
11. Linear Relations			C	
12. Negative Numbers	A			
Revision Exercises				R
13. Symmetry		B		
14. Bread and Butter Arithmetic	A			
15. Surveying		B		
Puzzle Corner, Revision				R
	7	5	3	4

BOOK 2

1. Topology		B			
2. Statistics			C		
3. Similarity and Enlargement		B			
4. Order and Punctuation	A				
Revision Exercises				R	
5. Reflection and Rotation		B			
6. Number Patterns	A				
7. Translations and Vectors		B			
Revision Exercises				R	
8. Relations and Functions			C		
9. The Slide Rule	A				
10. Solids		B			
11. Ratio and Proportion	A				
Revision Exercises				R	
12. Trigonometry		B			
13. Equations and Orderings	A				
14. Pythagoras' Theorem			C		
Puzzle Corner, Revision				R	
	5	6	3	4	

BOOK 3

1. Probability			C		
2. Isometries		B			
3. Matrices	A				
4. Rates of Change			C		
Revision Exercises				R	
5. The Circle		B			
6. Networks (relations)			C		
7. Three Dimensional Geometry		B			
8. Linear Programming			C		
Revision Exercises				R	
9. Waves		B			
10. Functions and Equations			C		
11. Identity and Inverse	A				
12. Shearing		B			
Revision Exercises				R	
13. Statistics			C		
14. Computers and Programming	A				
15. Loci and Envelopes		B			
	3	6	6	4	

BOOK 4

	A	B	C	R
1. Matrices and Transformations		B		
2. Solutions of Equations			C	
3. Trigonometry		B		
4. Logarithms	A			
Revision Exercises				R
5. Isometries		B		
6. Thinking Statistically			C	
7. Networks (Topology)		B		
Revision Exercises				R
8. Searching for Functions			C	
9. Co-ordinates in 3 Dimensions			C	
10. Structure and Equations	A			
11. Proportion, Rates of Change			C	
Revision Exercises				R
12. Vector Geometry		B		
13. Probability			C	
14. Geometry, Conclusions from data		B		
15. Computation	A			
	3	6	6	4

BOOK 5

	A	B	C	R
1. Areas and Graphs			C	
2. Vectors and Trigonometry		B		
3. The Sphere		B		
4. Functions and Graphs			C	
5. Practical Arithmetic	A			
6. Invariants in Geometry		B		
7. Plans and Elevations		B		
8. Linear Programming			C	
Review Chapters				
9. Structure	A			R
10. Co-ordinates and Mappings			C	R
11. Computation	A			R
12. Statistics and Probability			C	R
13. Geometry		B		R
14. Matrices	A	B	C	R
Miscellaneous Revision Exercises				R
	4	6	6	7

SUMMARY OF THE COURSE

	A	B	C	R
Book 1	7	5	3	4
Book 2	5	6	3	4
Book 3	3	6	6	4
Book 4	3	6	6	4
Book 5	4*	6*	6*	7*
	22*	29*	24*	23*
*Includes Review Chapters.	3	2	3	6

It will be noted that the first year has a preponderance of work on Sets and Number Theory to ensure a sound basis for further work; the second year gives prominence to Geometry; and the third and fourth years to Geometry, Relations and Graphs. The emphasis in these latter two years is on the cultural aspects of mathematics, and its utility as a tool for other subjects and for further developments in Mathematics itself. This is the kind of emphasis we would expect for the more able students. Book 5 seems to incorporate much of the traditional mathematics which had previously been neglected but now was seen to be desirable! And the final emphasis on a firm revision drawing together all the strands of the course, is designed to take up the whole of the last half year prior to the O-level examination which it is expected all candidates will take.

This course should be compared and contrasted with a course called *Making Mathematics* by D. Paling, C. S. Banwell and K. D. Saunders which is written specifically for children in the *lower ability range* in secondary schools, the 'slow learners' or 'backward children'. Here the structure of the course is even more clearly defined. Work is divided under four main headings, *Shape*, *Number*, *Measure*, *Topics and Investigations*. By reading across the page the development of the work under each of these main headings is seen. By reading down the columns in order, the actual sequence of the material is seen.

Because the children for whom this series is intended have limited attention and retention spans, and need the encouragement of success in attaining limited objectives, work has been arranged in small units taking about a week. In this way children are involved in Shape, Number, Measure, and usually a special Topic or Investigation together with some review each month.

By the time they get to Book 4 the children are much older, so the plan of the book is significantly different, as is seen by the arrangement outlined below. Work is now arranged in chapters to alternate

65

PLAN OF BOOK 1

	Looking at Shapes 3-D	The faces of some shapes	Lines of symmetry	Circles and circle patterns	'Four in a line' A co-ordinate game	Points and shapes on a grid	How shapes grow / Square numbers
Shape	Looking at Shapes 3-D	The faces of some shapes	Lines of symmetry	Circles and circle patterns	'Four in a line' A co-ordinate game	Points and shapes on a grid	How shapes grow / Square numbers
Number	Number squares $(+, -)$	Ready reckoners $(\times, \div)$	Finding the Number $(+, -, \times, \div)$	Number systems	Number patterns	'Where does the ball go' A modulo game	Using brackets
Measure	24-hour clock Isotypes and bar graphs	Length	Fractional parts	Angles and direction	Measuring angles	Distance ready reckoners	Idea of area Tessellations
Topics and Investigations		The Post Office (money, weight)		Milk at school and home (money, capacity)	The Baker (money, weight)	Travel and transport (money, weight)	
Reviews		R1, R2	R3, R4		R5, R6		R7, R8, R9

Note. At the end of the book there is a section *Some activities*. These are individual or group activities which can be used throughout the year

PLAN OF BOOK 2

Shape	Shapes from folding	Tiling patterns	Putting shapes into 'frames'	Lines and points	Intersecting circles	Constructions	Points on a square grid	Statistical investigations
Measure	Length Estimation and Approximation	Area	Volume	Angle properties of polygons	Fractions	Decimal fractions	Angles and length	Probability
Number	Number bases	Number bases $(+, -)$	Ready reckoners $(\times, \div)$	Relationships Arrow graphs	Our number system at work	More arrow graphs Envelopes	'Nines' Magic squares The '15' game	
Topics and Investigations	Decorating (money, capacity)	A drawing game	Gardening (money, weight, area)	A shape with a twist	Car ferry services (money, length, time)		A trihexaflexagon	
Reviews	R1, R2,	R3, R4	R5, R6	R7, R8	R9, R10	R11, R12	R13, R14, R15, R16	

Note. At the end of the book there is a section *Some activities*. These are individual or group activities which can be used throughout the year. There are also two pages of interesting puzzles.

PLAN OF BOOK 3

Shape	Symmetry Line and rotational	Drawing and making shapes	Polygons and the circle π	Making shapes larger and smaller	How high is it? Scale	Different points of view Plans and elevations	Some more models
Number	A calculating device Napier's bones	Relationships □, △ statements	Fractions (+, −)	Another calculating device Slide rule	Graphing relations Discrete	Functional situations Finding and graphing	Graphing relations Continuous
Measure	Computers Binary numbers	Metric system (length, money)	Statistics Grouped data	Averages Arithmetic mean, mode	A 2-state system Punched cards	Powers of numbers	Conversion graphs
Topics and Investigations	Number games	Line patterns	Routes	Numbers around us	The hexagon	Matchstick problems	
Reviews	R1, R2	R3, R4	R5, R6	R7, R8	R9, R10	R11, R12	

Note. At the end of the book there is a further page of *Activities*.

with work in Topic Books of which there are twelve. However for those who cannot yet retain an interest in a topic for such a prolonged period, each chapter *does* provide several natural breaks so that the whole chapter need not be completed at a first reading. The topic books each contain material on one particular topic and are written so that pairs or individuals can work on it. The material is arranged so that choices are provided at each stage.

PLAN OF BOOK 4

Two state systems	routes: probability 'trees': probability: Pascal's triangle: applications; *Pascal*
Pythagoras	tessellations leading to the theorem: squares and square roots: applications: *Pythagoras*
Speeding up calculations	properties of numbers/operations: nomograms (length/width/perimeter, length/width/area)
Number patterns	activities related to Pascal's triangle: sequences (including Fibonacci): digit sums
Distance, time, speed	average speed: use of nomogram: units of speed: special units
Networks	unicursal routes: Euler's rules related to networks and polyhedra: matrices for describing networks: applications
Random numbers, area, volume	randomness: area of squares, irregular shapes, circles: volume of prisms (including cylinders)
Statistics	interpretation of tables and graphs: investigations: correlation (scattergrams): permutations (competitions)
Plans and maps	enlargement and scale: plane-table survey ordnance survey maps: similar shapes (2-D and 3-D), relationships between length/area/volume: applications
Using formulae	investigations leading to the use of formulae: formulae for area, volume, speed, etc.
Some activities	

1. Sampling and Probability 2. Movement and Pattern
3. Making Models 4. Practical Design
5. Living on a Sphere 6. Creative Design
7. Flow diagrams to computers 8. Mathematical Games
9. What Can You Earn 10. What Can You Spend?
11. Best Buy 12. Using Tables

It is instructive to note both the similarites and the differences of these two courses catering as they do for pupils from the two extremes of ability. Quite clearly the SMP course contains many more topics and these are pursued to a far greater depth. There is also in the SMP course much more emphasis on the cultural and developmental aspects of mathematics, the kind of mathematics required of those going on to further education; while in the latter course there is much greater emphasis on numerical work, on measure, and other 'utilitarian aims'.

However it will be noted that there is a broad measure of similarity; a somewhat similar balance for in the second course the 'Topics and Investigations' together with some of the items included under 'Number' correspond to the 'Relations and Graphs' categorisation in the analysis of the SMP course. And both agree fairly closely in overall content with the proposed outline on page 59.

Although we are anticipating the substance of later chapters, both also imply individual and group work as teaching techniques; both build in aspects of *challenge* but also ensure *likelihood of success*; both introduce games, puzzles, unusual problems, historical incidents, and other activities that ensure variety; and both exude a sense of enthusiasm and enjoyment which is infectious. In so far as they are successful in these respects they represent the spirit of 'modern mathematics'.

Summary
This chapter has been concerned chiefly with the third aspect of the teaching process, *content* which follows after Goals and Objectives. In determining the content we have had to look not only to the mathematical desirability of including certain topics, but also their interrelationship in order to create an effective *scheme*. We have recognised the principle that the content will be varied according to the ability and needs of the pupil but have tried to set out an overall

scheme from which items can be deleted, and in the case of the very able, to which other items could be added. We recognise too that no course is going to succeed, no matter how well defined the content, if appropriate strategies and methods are not used in the actual teaching.

5. Strategy

In the last chapter we considered the question of what to teach. This chapter and the next go on to consider the associated question, 'How do we teach it?' In the preliminary chapter the distinction was drawn between *strategy* and *method*, where strategy referred to the overall approach to a topic or area of study, and method to the actual process of applying this approach in a definite situation.

Strategy then is the wider concept, and in our discussion it will be well to bear in mind three major aspects of it. The first concerns differences of approach that will be necessary because of the differences of ability, background and attitude of the children. The second concerns the recognition that there are a variety of different *kinds* of learning, or *stages* within the learning process, each requiring a different strategy. The third arises from the fact that for any given topic there are frequently different approaches possible from a purely mathematical point of view.

Differences in student ability

Our first consideration is the very marked differences we will find amongst our students. These differences are likely to be very considerable on arrival at the secondary school, and to get progressively *more marked*. Differences in mental ability, the ability to reason or think reflectively and to solve problems, in so far as they are innate rather than through lack of appropriate background and instruction, must result in increasingly divergent levels of attainment if each child is encouraged to work to the best of his ability. So any school programme should make provision for this diversity, rather than try to cover it up by giving the same curriculum to all.

Apart from general ability, or IQ, there are specific mathematical factors, the ability to use symbols, to do logical reasoning, to compute with accuracy and speed, and to appreciate spatial relationships. Here again we may be misled at first because the knowledge of mathematical concepts, structures and processes is related very much to the previous educational experience of the learner and largely determines his readiness for the content of the new course.

In addition to these differences which are to some extent measurable by various tests, there are other differences for which at present there is very little to help the teacher – motivations, interests, attitudes and appreciations, all of which have an important bearing on the classroom situation. Some of these are dependent on the physical, emotional, and social maturity of the learner. All of these factors bear an important part in assessing the placement of children in special classes. Of course any real physical disability should be noted, and its effect on the child's emotional reactions should be watched; and minor defects in sensory perception such as in sight or hearing should be ascertained and appropriate provision made.

Some students may have special talents, such as a creative flair, or special deficiencies such as a lack of reading skill; and these again will have a major bearing on the type of work that it is appropriate for the child to pursue. Then there will be differences of learning habits, self-discipline, attention and retention span, and organisation of written work. These are frequently related to the child's home background and previous education.

Naturally these differences will be taken into account in some degree by the overall school structure. For example, there may be *streaming*, or *banding*, or *setting*. These involve issues far wider than just the teaching of mathematics. However their effect can be considerable. It may well happen, in fact, that within a single school there are different courses, and even different *kinds* of course offered. These courses may be based on a textbook (or textbook series) probably supplemented by topic books or other material designed to enrich the experience of the learner. Alternatively it may be decided to base some or all the course on a series of topics or projects. These would spring from the interests and concerns of students and would include work which related to other disciplines such as science, geography, metalwork, and so on. Or it may be decided that as far as possible *all* instruction should be based on individual and group assignments which for their working depend on all the recent technological resources available: programmed learning both by texts and machines, film loops, slides, full feature films, instructions on tape, as well as ordinary assignment cards, both individual and group. This last kind of approach will probably only be possible in experimental schools, or schools for the very wealthy; and certainly will apply to only a limited number of schools even in developed countries like Britain or the U.S.A.

However, whatever the total school situation, the place where these considerations are most likely to hit the teacher is going to be *within* the class or classes to which he is assigned. There, the larger problem of the whole school becomes his own special problem. For no matter what overall school organisation there is, and what attempts there are to provide a homogeneous group of approximately equal ability (if such attempts are made at all) there will always be considerable variation in ability amongst the students in a single class.

One of the most common ways of dealing with this problem is by varying the daily learning assignments according to ability or achievement levels. So in a typical situation a certain number of questions or exercises will be set which it is expected that *everyone* will do and the more capable are given either *more* problems to do, or *more difficult* and challenging problems to do, or both. In many textbooks provision of this kind is made by placing asterisks against questions that are more difficult. This procedure is supplemented by ensuring that while students are working on their own, the teacher goes round to give individual assistance of whatever kind is required. This not infrequently reveals that a certain idea has not been understood by a large number of the class, and that reteaching is necessary!

Unfortunately it often happens that teachers feel that this is *all* that is required of them, and their instruction becomes stifled in formalism. So other ways must be sought. One way is to use 'enrichment topics' such as students reports, displays and creative writing, where different standards of assessment can be applied according to the known abilities of the students. These offer a useful outlet for meeting the problem of differences in ability. For some purposes the class can be organised into small groups according to ability and each group given special instructions and assignments. This technique is often very valuable when a set of models is required for later class discussion. The less able are given the simpler models to prepare, the more able the more complicated. But *all* the models will be used in the corporate discussion later, and everyone will have a sense of having contributed something useful for the class as a whole.

In other cases, the grouping may be done on a slightly different basis and for a different reason, e.g. to conserve on resources. It may then be appropriate to appoint more capable students as group leaders. These students then get experience of leading and even teaching. Details of a series of lessons along these lines will be found on page 119.

Work of this kind gives students the experience of the use of work cards on a group basis and prepares them for a second stage – the use of cards for students working in small groups of two or three or even individually. This enables children to work at their own speed at tasks which are appropriate to their own ability.

If a teacher has not used work cards before a good way to begin is to write individual assignment cards as an alternative to the asterisked problems in an exercise referred to earlier on. When a student has completed the required work set to the whole class he is given an individual card to get on with. This can either consist of harder examples of the same kind like 'starred' problems; or alternatively be something quite different, a personal investigation or problem, a puzzle, a paradox, something to challenge the mind. On the other hand, additional examples of a simpler variety could be given to pupils who need extra practice to consolidate an idea without any further complications (see Fig. 45).

Fairly early on, if this idea is pursued, it will be necessary to develop a filing system so that cards can be brought out and used again. A possible way would be to give a heading fixing the text, chapter and exercise to which it is tied, and then a code, say P – problems of a more difficult kind, puzzles, and paradoxes; A – additional problems of the same standard for extra practice; S – simple exercises for remedial purposes. Another useful idea is to cover the card with acetate or a material like *Transpaseal*, which, while smooth on one side, has an adhesive surface on the other. This not only gives protection and longer life to the card, but allows students to write in answers on the card using a water-based felt pen which can easily be wiped off before the card is given to another student.

A later stage is to write on the card an instruction like that shown in Fig. 46. Such a card not only encourages individual work but gets

MODERN ALGEBRA, VOL II
Page 96, Exercise III
Supplementary work, P1
....
....

Fig. 45.

Fig. 46.

SUPPLEMENTARY WORK
TOPIC: BINARY NUMBER SYSTEM P2
Find: RIDDLES IN MATHEMATICS
          by Eugene Northrop
Read pages 31–38

students reading books from the library for enjoyment. It may well happen, that stimulated by the section on Binary Number the student will go on to read a good deal more in the book besides. In addition to books of general interest like that referred to, there are now some excellent *Topic* books meant for individual study by students, distributed by a number of publishers, e.g.

Exploring mathematics on your own – John Murray
Exploring mathematics   – Grant
Experiments in mathematics   – Longmans
Further experiments in mathematics – Longmans
Making mathematics topic books   – Oxford University Press
Topics from mathematics   – Cambridge University Press

A number of these titles should be in the Mathematics room (or library) and available for student use.

As an alternative to work cards we may decide to refer individual students to a programmed textbook. Such a book is designed to present material to a reader in a series of short steps. These steps consist of a brief exposition followed by a question or questions to which the reader responds usually by writing the answer in the space provided. The reader then checks his answer against those supplied in the book (often hidden by a slide, or presented on some other page). The questions provide the learner with immediate knowledge of his progress. In some programmes, called branching programmes, incorrect answers may direct the reader to remedial work, but the most important function of the question and answer process is the deeper involvement of the reader in the learning activity. He is virtually forced by the questions to share responsibility for learning. Moreover as the student reacts to each question he is led to discover a generalisation, and as answers are given to each question or problem, correct answers are reinforced, and mistakes are put right straight away. Two useful series of texts of this kind are the following:

Clearway Programmed Books – Methuen
Discovery Programmes   – Longmans

Theoretically, programmed textbooks seem to be an ideal way of providing for individual differences. The slow learner goes at a rate appropriate to him while the quick can forge ahead. Also they are useful for students to make up work missed during an absence, or for remedial instruction if this is necessary.

However, it has been found that if programmed texts are used too much they tend to prove monotonous, especially for slow learners to work at independently day after day writing answers to questions. Even more is this true if there is any reading difficulty. On the other hand the talented student often finds that the questions seem trivial and time consuming. Nevertheless when used as a *part* of an overall programme they can be extremely valuable and be one more means of introducing variety with purpose, and of meeting individual needs.

Programmes are also written for use with machines. Here the unit of work is the *frame* which may be brought into view by winding a handle or manipulating a switch which releases a whole card. Increasingly modern technology is trying to harness film projectors, loops, tape recorders, etc. to give greater variety to programmes, to provide greater flexibility, to allow increasingly for individual differences, and in some experimental schools the *whole* mathematics programme is completely individualised, i.e. the students works on his own the *whole* time following a series of assignments allotted by the teacher. These assignments include work sheets, programmed texts, films, tape recorded sessions, discussion group work, model making and so on, and each is designed to meet the capabilities and interests of the pupil. There are, of course, immense difficulties of organisation and assessment in such a course, but those adopting such schemes speak highly of student attitudes towards mathematics.

In this section we have been stressing that one of the most important points of general strategy is to *cater for individual differences* in as wide a variety of ways as possible. We pass now to the second major aspect of strategy, the various differences in the kinds and stages of learning.

Different learning processes
One of the points made in the previous section was the need for *variety* and for providing for individual differences. One of the chief reasons for arguing along these lines is that only thus are we likely to promote positive attitudes towards mathematics. Another way of doing this, and one that is associated very much with 'modern methods' is the investigation.

The Investigation
The investigation is essentially work done by the student on his own or perhaps with a friend, and its purpose is to instil a willingness to

come to grips with real problems with confidence and originality, and to see increasingly how mathematical methods are applied to a variety of problems.

This is a case where students have to be led gradually. At first 'investigation' cards will not be very different from 'experimental' or other work cards that may be used in other connections. The examples below show the general sort of development one might expect from cards in the first instance where practically every step is detailed to those where a problem or topic is only suggested or out-

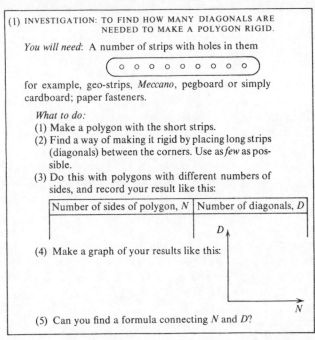

(1) INVESTIGATION: TO FIND HOW MANY DIAGONALS ARE NEEDED TO MAKE A POLYGON RIGID.

You will need: A number of strips with holes in them

for example, geo-strips, *Meccano*, pegboard or simply cardboard; paper fasteners.

What to do:
(1) Make a polygon with the short strips.
(2) Find a way of making it rigid by placing long strips (diagonals) between the corners. Use as *few* as possible.
(3) Do this with polygons with different numbers of sides, and record your result like this:

Number of sides of polygon, N	Number of diagonals, D

(4) Make a graph of your results like this:

(5) Can you find a formula connecting N and D?

---

(2) INVESTIGATION OF SPEED AND STOPPING DISTANCES

You will need the following information taken from the Highway Code (Great Britain):

Speed (mph)	20	30	40	50	60	70
Thinking distance (ft)	20	30	40	50	60	70
Braking distance (ft)	20	45	80	125	180	245
Overall stopping distance (ft)	40	75	120	175	240	315

What to do: Examine the figures above and then draw graphs to show any relationships that may exist.

> (3) INVESTIGATION OF TRIANGLES OF CONSTANT
> PERIMETER
>
> *You will need*: A loop of string 30 cm long; 2 drawing
> pins, set square, cartridge paper, and graph paper.
>
> *What to do*: Using the string as perimeter, investigate
> (1) Triangles with a fixed base (the distance between
>   two pins)
> (2) Right angled triangles
> (3) Isosceles triangles

> (4) INVESTIGATION OF AREAS AND PERIMETERS OF
> TRIANGLES
>
> Under what conditions are the area and perimeter of
> a triangle numerically equal?
> Are there extensions to other polygons?

lined. The final investigations may, in fact, prove of interest to the reader!

The examples above are indicative of a general principle of strategy concerning 'discovery methods'. This is *not to tell* students things that they can reasonably find out for themselves, either directly or as a result of question and answer. The process of *telling* makes the learners passive recipients; the process of *finding out* makes them active learners. This applies not only to material developed through work cards, but also to 'formal' lessons. When a child makes a 'discovery', his whole attitude is changed. He gains in confidence and understanding; he shows excitement and interest and this leads to curiosity about other relationships. One of the most powerful ways of doing this is to constantly stress the search for *pattern*, which is why graphical methods are so good for finding relationships between quantities or measures. But patterns arise in other connections too, and not least in number work, in algebraic structures, and of course geometry. We turn now to an associated activity, problem solving.

Problem solving
The principles of teaching problem solving are best illustrated by a particular example. Fig. 47 represents a 'street' map of a modern town. Starting at *A*, how many 'sensible' ways are there of reaching any other intersection like *B*? Such a problem can either be put on a work card for individual or group investigation or be used for class discussion.

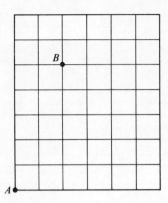

Fig. 47.

The first job of course is to make sure that the problem is understood, and in doing this we shall certainly want to define what is 'sensible'! After we have looked at examples of 'sensible' and 'not-sensible' routes, we may find that in this particular case 'sensible' is equivalent to 'shortest', and it may come as a bit of a shock to find that there are, in general, several shortest ways of going from *A* to *B*.

Inevitably – and it is important that this be realised – the next step is to take a number of points *at random*, and by *trial and error* find out the number of ways of reaching it. At this stage, our diagram may look something like Fig. 48. This trial and error period is essential. It gives you a *feeling* for the problem; it enables you to see what the difficulties are.

Sooner or later some desire for order will make us want to start in a systematic way, beginning with the *simplest cases* and working towards the more complicated. Our diagram after a bit of work along these lines may reach a stage like that shown in Fig. 49.

At around this stage the *pattern* will become obvious, and it will be *noticed* that the figure for any vertex is the *sum* of the figure to the

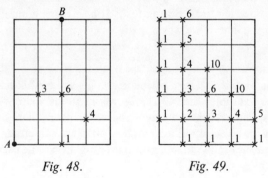

Fig. 48.   *Fig. 49.*

80

left of it and the figure below it. Alternatively, depending on the experience of the investigator it may be noticed that these are the figures of *Pascal's Triangle*, though not set out in quite the conventional way.

The question now is, 'Can we justify or explain these results?' Clearly we can. If there are n ways of reaching P there are also n ways of reaching B through P (Fig. 50). Likewise if there are m ways of reaching Q there are m ways of reaching B through Q. As we can only reach B by going through either P or Q, there must be $(m + n)$ ways of reaching B.

For those who have done the Binomial Theorem and work on permutations and combinations there will be a final step, that of wishing

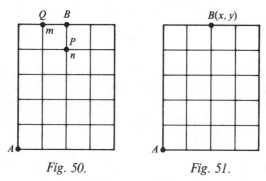

Fig. 50.   *Fig. 51.*

to summarise and prove a general result. If B has co-ordinates (x, y) (Fig. 51) then the required number of ways, N is given by the formula:

$$N = {}^{(x+y)}C_x \text{ or } {}^{(x+y)}C_y$$

This is explained by showing that at any vertex there is the choice of going *up* (or North) or *sideways* (or East). To reach B we have had to take x steps East, and y steps North, i.e. to make $(x+y)$ decisions and from these choose x East and y North, and the number of ways of doing this is precisely ${}^{(x+y)}C_x$ (or ${}^{(x+y)}C_y$).

The important thing about this example is what it tells us about problems and the way we tackle them. This may be summarised by the flow chart in Fig. 52. A 'good' problem (and those from everyday life) is usually stated fairly *simply* to begin with in language that is not too precise. Very often we have to rephrase it giving *definitions* to terms so that there can be no ambiguity. The language aspect of mathematics is here very evident.

81

If the problem is completely new we try a number of approaches looking for any that look more hopeful than others. If no immediate success is attained, we resort next to trying to do things in a systematic way all the time looking for patterns and likenesses to situations or problems we have come across before. Experience here is very important. Hopefully there will then come a moment of insight when the problem is either solved or at least the method of attack is clear. We must then use mathematical techniques to complete the solution or justify our insight by giving logical mathematical reasons for our intuition. The genuine mathematician then tries to go one stage further and see if there is any further generalisation possible. I feel that the following steps need stressing:

(1) That *time* is necessary for trial and error in order for a genuine appreciation of the problem to be made. How often we present a problem, knowing the answer, and proceed to the 'justification' before our students have even appreciated what they are being asked to do! Very often this step requires the use of concrete apparatus, visual aids, etc. that students can handle and manipulate themselves.

(2) That discovery is more likely to those with better background. They have more links, more patterns, more similarities, more techniques to fall back on. Certain patterns, particularly those of linear and inverse (hyperbolic) relations are so important that we should make sure they form part of the background to any student's thinking. Likewise the techniques of algebra and the ability to formulate equations is an essential tool.

(3) The genuine mathematician is going to show himself in his urge to move on to generalisation. The vast majority will be content with the solution to the original problem!

A final point before we leave 'the problem' – the 'best' problems are ones that can be easily *understood*, but require a wide range of initiative to solve. Such problems are hard to find, and if found are worth preserving (see note on p. 105).

Although problems and investigations form an important part of anyone's mathematical education, it must be recognised that equally important are two other areas – the formulation of *concepts*, and the development of *skills*. Both of these in fact frequently *precede* any serious problem solving for part of the job of problem solving is to relate the problem to concepts already known and held; and any strategy or plan one adopts for solving problems depends on the skills and techniques available to one.

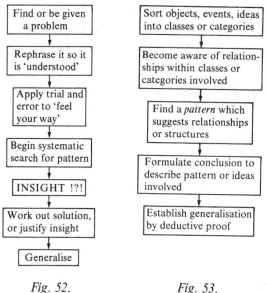

Fig. 52. Fig. 53.

Forming concepts

Concepts are mental abstractions of common properties of a set of experiences or phenomena. We cannot properly grasp such an 'abstraction' until we have seen the property in a number of different circumstances. So in the most elementary case, we cannot get the concept of *red* until we have seen a large number of objects all coloured red and have been able to *recognise* this quality of alikeness in all the objects concerned. There is a genuine difficulty here for the colour-blind.

Mathematical concepts have as their basis, sets. These sets may involve objects, operations, relations, or structures. In every case, however, there seems to be a common process, which is represented in Fig. 53.

The first step is sorting objects, events, or ideas into classes or categories. In the early stages of secondary school, this sorting means the actual handling of physical objects, just as it has in the primary school. To use the terminology of Piaget, most children are still in the *concrete operational stage* and are not yet ready for the abstract operational stage where the 'objects' of our sorting are themselves often concepts previously acquired.

The second step is to become aware of relationships within the classes or categories involved. This implies that there has been sufficient background experience for this awareness to develop. In the primary school, for example, we talk about *number readiness*, i.e. a sufficient background of handling concrete sets of objects to realise that the matching operation of which number is built is meaningful and useful. There must also be a willingness on the part of the student for this awareness must develop *within him*; it cannot be imposed from outside. This willingness will result from a good class atmosphere, a sense of involvement and of security, and from a knowledge that the teacher is concerned about him and his progress. This last point is of fundamental importance, for if the student gets the idea that he is of no significance to the teacher or community, then there is clearly no reason why he should be willing to participate in anything, far less put himself out to learn anything!

The third stage of *finding a pattern* corresponds very closely to the stage preceding *insight* in problem solving. It implies a native ability on the part of the student. Some students can reach this point with very little guidance. Others need far more, and indeed the elements of the pattern may have to be brought into very close juxtaposition in order for the pattern to be 'seen'. But the crucial point is that in some sense at least the pattern is 'found' by the child, that something is required from him, that he must think. He must not fall into the attitude of expecting always to be told.

When a pattern has been recognised we must try *not* to be content with the pattern but to formulate a conclusion which describes the pattern of events or ideas involved. A good example is work on paper folding, 'ink blot' drawings and other experiences leading to the idea of line symmetry (Fig. 54). The symmetry is often recognised: 'It's the same on both sides.' What is now required is a discussion of what is meant by that simple statement. We need to draw out in discussion

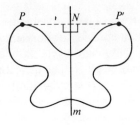

Fig. 54.

the idea of object P and image P' and show that 'the same' implies that

length of PN = length of $P'N$

and $\quad PP' \perp m$

or summarising that for *any* point P and its image P', m (the axis of symmetry) is the mediator or perpendicular bisector of PP'.

The final stage now of formalising or generalising by deductive proof would include showing that for any point P the image P' is unique.

Again from the point of view of the teacher it is essential to realise how important the first stage is, the handling of materials, *time* to get used to the objects or ideas involved so that similarities *can* be noticed. It is important, too, to realise that in the case of eventually abstracting a concept like *group structure*, a number of *different* sets of circumstances in which the structure is revealed form the necessary background. All this may take a long time, possibly several terms. But of course group structure is not the only reason for including much of the work in transformation geometry, finite arithmetics and so on. It does, however, provide an eventual unifying thread.

Learning skills

Skills usually concern the repeated application of certain mathematical concepts which are found to be useful in a variety of situations. Thus training in skills should normally *follow* the acquiring of a concept. Put another way, we first teach *understanding* and then *if the concept is needed sufficiently often*, we refine our methods to find the most economic and satisfactory way of performing a series of operations and thus develop a skill. The order again is important, for to develop a skill with no understanding either of the concepts involved or the applications for which the skill is required is deadly.

The logical development as far as possible appears to be the following: First develop concepts, then pose problems that use these concepts, and show that in solving problems of this kind, certain skills will be useful. Thus the reason for acquiring the skill will be appreciated and there will be adequate motivation.

A skill is acquired, in the first instance, by a large amount of repetitive practice. It is here that large numbers of exercises of the same kind play an important part. The exercises themselves must be understood to be serving this purpose and not necessarily to have any other great significance.

A comparison with music may serve a purpose. One of the basic skills required by a competent pianist is to be able to run up or down a succession of notes whenever it occurs in a piece of music. So important is this that pianists spend hours playing *scales*. The scales, themselves, do not have any great significance musically, but the ability to play them fluently and accurately when required in the body of a musical score is of the greatest importance to a proper rendering of a great deal of worth-while music. In the same way, many of the manipulative skills and techniques of algebra and trigonometry find their significance not in themselves, but in the fact that they contribute to the understanding and solution of more complex and important mathematical problems.

The comparison with music can perhaps be taken a stage further. Although at a certain stage in a pianist's development a vast amount of time must be spent on the playing of scales to *attain* fluency, once that fluency is obtained it is not necessary to *continue* to spend so much time on them provided that they are maintained by constant use either in compositions that include them or by short regular practice sessions. The same is true of mathematical skills. Once acquired they must be maintained either by constant use in the solution of problems or by periodic revision and practice.

The place of memory work

Much the same sort of remarks may be made about memory work as about skills. Those results, formulae, relationships which occur sufficiently often to make it worth-while are committed to memory as a saving of time, and an increase in efficiency. However, since the work is built on *understanding* first, if the memory should fail, then one can have recourse to finding the relationship again from first principles. It is clear that amongst the facts that one requires everyone to know are the 'number-bonds' or the addition and multiplication facts concerning numbers up to 10×10. As to the eleven and twelve times tables, some will consider them worthwhile memorising, others that they will occur so infrequently once we move to metric measure that it is sufficient when they do so, to apply the distributive law:

e.g. $8 \times 12 = 8(10 + 2) = 80 + 16 = 96$

All these steps, of course, would be carried out mentally.

The purpose of the foregoing discussion is to establish the fact that *strategy* demands that we acknowledge not only differences in pupils but also differences in method arising from different stages in the learning process, whether it be original investigations, problem solving, the acquisition of new mathematical concepts, or the development and maintenance of skills. The *purpose*, therefore, of each lesson or group of lessons must be clearly before us as we plan them. We come now to the final point of strategy as applied to different learning processes, the control of progress.

Controlling progress

An essential feature of all that has been said so far is that as we have got a variety of different students involved at different times in different learning processes achieved at different rates, the whole activity can be prodigiously wasteful if there is not a definite and ordered scheme of work, a programme that ensures that every student is making controlled progress. This is true whether we adopt a very 'formal' situation or a 'free' one; one based largely on a textbook, or divorced entirely from a text and dependent on programmed learning using a variety of teaching aids as in the case below:

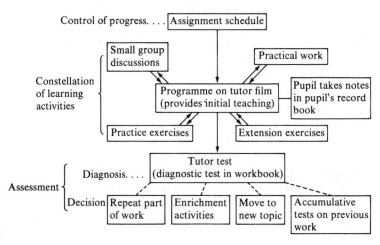

Fig. 55.

An examination of this scheme shows a number of important aspects of organisation (see Fig. 55). Central to the development is the 'assignment schedule' which in a conventional situation would be called the 'scheme of work'. Then a topic is developed, and in this case the initial phase is the programme on tutor film. This corresponds to an introduction or explanation by the teacher. Such work is only the beginning. There are then what are referred to as the 'constellation of learning activities', practical work, discussions, practice exercises and extension exercises which provide the *variety* we have been referring to previously, and which are clearly modified according to the needs and abilities of the students. There then comes some sort of evaluation as a result of which a decision is taken as to whether to repeat the work, progress to a new topic, engage in an enrichment activity, or go back to some previously learned work in a cumulative review. When the decision is taken to move to a new topic the cycle is repeated and hence the learning is at all times both directed and controlled. It provides then a convenient summary to basic teaching strategy.

There remains, however, one last aspect of strategy and this relates to the *material itself*. Even when all the previous considerations have been taken into account, there may be more than one perfectly logical, consistent, and practical approach to the teaching of certain topics. Some examples of this are given in the succeeding section.

Different approaches to selected topics
In this section we shall take a few topics and consider a variety of approaches or strategies that could be used to teach them. The treatment will not be detailed, nor will it claim to be exhaustive, but merely illustrative of the general principle that one should be aware of the possibility of variety in approach. In particular the plea is made that, when a textbook is used, the strategy should be carefully considered to see whether it is the most appropriate for the class or individual students concerned.

Multiplication of Directed Numbers
One of the most frequent questions in elementary algebra is 'Why does a negative times a negative give a positive product?' To try to answer this question a variety of strategies such as the following are used.

(1) Relate the multiplication process to trips on the number line. This will extend the visualisation of the multiplication process used previously. The new elements here are the idea of positive and negative directions, positive and negative time, and positive and negative distance.

Suppose that John lives on a road running East–West. Consider the road as a number line with John's house as origin, distances East as positive and West negative. Likewise a car travelling eastwards will be thought of as moving positively; one travelling westwards as moving negatively. Future time is called positive and past time negative, the present being zero. (Note how many conditions must be established for this 'intuitive' development!)

Then $(^+30)(^+2) = {}^+60$ since travel eastwards at 30 mph for 2 hours in the future results in arriving 60 miles east of John's house. How then would the following be interpreted?

$$(^-30)(^+2) = {}^-60$$
$$(^+30)(^-2) = {}^-60$$

Finally $(^-30)(^-2) = {}^+60$ means that a car travelling westwards at 30 mph *was* 60 miles east of John's house two hours ago.

(2) A somewhat simpler version consists of drawing two cars pointed in positive and negative directions, and considering the direction of motion when the driver engages a forward gear (+), or reverse gear (−).

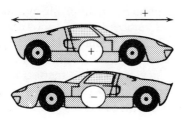

Fig. 56.

(3) Income and expenditure resulting in being 'in the red' and 'in the black' give another application.

(4) The UICSM (University of Illinois Committee on School Mathematics) group in America uses the ingenious method of a motion picture projector which runs forward (+) or backward (−). Then a film run forward of a pump filling (+) or draining (−) a tank will result in an increase (+) or decrease (−) of liquid in the tank respectively. When the film is reversed, the opposite will be true.

(5) A different strategy uses patterns for *predicting* the product on an initial assumption that $(^+a)(^+b) = {}^+ab$

$$\begin{aligned}
\text{Consider} \quad (^+3)(^+2) &= {}^+6 \\
(^+3)(^+1) &= {}^+3 \\
(^+3)(\ 0) &= \ 0 \\
(^+3)(^-1) &= \ ? \\
(^+3)(^-2) &= \ ?
\end{aligned}$$

When $(^+3)(^-2) = {}^-6$ is established and accepted, use the commutative property and proceed:

$$(^-2)(^+3) = {}^-6$$
$$(^-2)(^+2) = {}^-4$$
$$(^-2)(^+1) = {}^-2$$
$$(^-2)(\ 0) = \ \ 0$$
$$(^-2)(^-1) = \ \ ?$$

(6) This can be done more directly by assigning the meaning of repeated addition to a positive first term; of repeated subtraction to a negative first term. Thus:

$(^+3)(^+2)$ is interpreted as *add* $(^+2)$ three times. Result $^+6$.
$(^+3)(^-2)$ is interpreted as *add* $(^-2)$ three times. Result $^-6$.
$(^-3)(^+2)$ is interpreted as *subtract* $(^+2)$ three times. Result $^-6$.
$(^-3)(^-2)$ is interpreted as *subtract* $(^-2)$ three times. Result $^+6$.

(7) A graphical approach of multiplying by a positive number, say $^+2$ using two parallel number lines will show that we can associate the multiplicative $^+2$ with a definite point on the perpendicular line passing through the zeros (see solid lines in Fig. 57). Clearly if we extend x to include negative values, there is no need to alter the point $(^+2)$ on the vertical line. We thus establish results for the product of positive and negative integers (see dotted lines in Fig. 57).

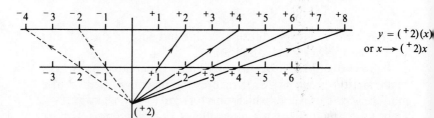

$$y = (^+2)(x)$$
$$\text{or } x \longrightarrow (^+2)x$$

Fig. 57.

Having learned that the product of a positive number and a negative number is a negative number, we can apply the process all over again and find, for example, the multiplicative point $^-2$ (see Fig. 58). This, in turn leads to the required result.

(8) A somewhat novel approach is to assign positive and negative signs to *areas* reflected in the axes in precisely the same way as we assign signs to points on the axes themselves (see Fig. 59). Thus the original area $A_0 = (^+4)(^+3) = {}^+12$. A reflection of A_0 in the y-axis

90

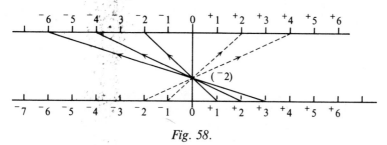

Fig. 58.

results in x being negative, and the area negative, i.e.:

$$A_1 = (^-4)(^+3) = {}^-12$$

Likewise a reflection of A_0 in the x-axis results in y being negative and the area being negative:

$$A_2 = (^+4)(^-3) = {}^-12$$

$(0, {}^+3)$

$A_1 = (^-4)(^+3)$
$\quad = {}^-12$

$A_0 = (^+4)(^+3)$
$\quad = {}^+12$

$(^-4,0)$

$(^+4,0)$

$A_2 = (^+4)(^-3)$
$\quad = {}^-12$

$(0, {}^-3)$

Fig. 59.

The question now is, 'What happens if we reflect A_1 in the x-axis, or A_2 in the y-axis?' There is, of course, a close parallel here to the way in which signs are allocated to cosine, sine and tangents in trigonometry; and with transformation geometry – two reflections being equivalent to a rotation.

(9) At a higher level a deductive approach is possible:

$(^+3)\cdot0 = 0$	Property of zero
$(^+3)(^+2 + {}^-2) = 0$	Substitution for zero
$(^+3)(^+2) + (^+3)(^-2) = 0$	Distributive property
$^+6 + (^+3)(^-2) = 0$	Assuming $(^+3)(^+2) = {}^+6$
$(^+3)(^-2) = {}^-6$	Both $(^+3)(^-2)$ and $^-6$ are additive inverses to $^+6$, or by adding $^-6$ to both sides.

Similarly in more general terms and starting with ^-a, we have:

$$^-a \cdot 0 = 0$$
$$^-a \cdot (^+b + {}^-b) = 0$$
$$^-ab + (^-a)(^-b) = 0$$
$$(^-a)(^-b) = {}^+ab$$

(10) All the illustrations 1–8 suffer from the basic difficulty that the respective numbers are not treated in the *same way*. Either one is a velocity, another a time; one a direction, another a gear; one an instruction to add or subtract, the other an 'ordinary' directed number; the numbers distances, the products areas. Ideally we have got to reach the stage when the two numbers and the product are all from the same set, and so we are led to the idea of ordered pairs of natural numbers to define integers, and new *definitions* for addition and multiplication which are consistent with previous understandings.

Initial work can be simplified if the ordered pairs are separated vertically instead of horizontally, i.e. $\binom{a}{b}$ rather than (a, b). The presentation can then be compared with work on fractions with its own rules for addition and multiplication. We make the assumptions that if $a > b$, the new quantity $\binom{a}{b}$ is regarded as positive, while if $b > a$, then $\binom{a}{b}$ is taken as negative, and say that $\binom{a}{b} = \binom{c}{d}$ if $a + d = b + c$.

Addition is then defined by: $\binom{a}{b} + \binom{c}{d} = \binom{a+c}{b+d}$ and

multiplication by: $\binom{a}{b} \times \binom{c}{d} = \binom{ac + bd}{ad + bc}$

Though the definition for addition is fairly natural (and corresponds to that for vector addition), that for multiplication always seems far-fetched even after it has been shown to be consistent! But this should perhaps give us an insight into the inherent difficulty of dealing with fractions, where the law of combination for multiplication is simple, that for addition complex.

The choice of total strategy will probably include a number of these different approaches with a view ultimately of using either 9 or 10 or both.

Simultaneous linear equations
Initial work involves solving a *pair* of simultaneous equations, and a distinction probably has to be made between a strategy for *understanding*, and a strategy for *performing*. This may become clearer as we discuss the various approaches, and in particular consider ways of solving the following pair of simultaneous equations:

$$7x + 8y = 23$$
$$6x - 5y = -4$$

1. *Graphical*

The idea is to draw graphs of each 'equation' (function) separately and note their points of intersection. This has the merit of giving a visual impression of what's going on, and of wide applicability to the solution of simultaneous equations which are not necessarily linear (see also p. 55). However as a *technique* for the repeated solution of pairs of simultaneous linear equations it is most unsuitable, as it is time-consuming and frequently none too accurate.

2. *Substitution*

This method also has the merit that it stresses a technique of wider applicability, in particular when one of the equations is linear and the other is not. However in its application to a pair of simultaneous linear equations it sometimes leads to unnecessarily heavy manipulation.

$$7x + 8y = 23 \qquad \text{(i)}$$
$$6x - 5y = -4 \qquad \text{(ii)}$$

From (i) $\quad x = \dfrac{23 - 8y}{7} \qquad$ (iii)

Substituting in (ii): $\quad 6\left(\dfrac{23 - 8y}{7}\right) - 5y = -4$

$$138 - 48y - 35y = -28$$
$$166 = 83y$$
$$\left. \begin{array}{l} y = 2 \\ x = 1 \end{array} \right\}$$

Hence from (iii)

3. *Elimination*

This method stresses the logical point that equal quantities remain equal if they are treated in the same way.

$7x + 8y = 23$ (i)   Multiply both sides by 5: $35x + 40y = 115$ (iii)
$6x - 5y = -4$ (ii)   Multiply both sides by 8: $48x - 40y = -32$ (iv)

$$\begin{array}{rl} \text{Add (iii) and (iv)} & 83x = 83 \\ & x = 1 \\ \text{Hence} \quad & y = 2 \end{array}$$

Although this method is often found to be less convincing than the others, it is usually the easiest to follow through correctly and quickly.

4. *Matrix approach*

If the equation is written in the form $\mathbf{Mx} = \mathbf{a}$ and if further another matrix $\mathbf{M}^{-1}$ can be found so that $\mathbf{M}^{-1}\mathbf{M} = \mathbf{I}$, then we have a *general* method of solving systems of simultaneous linear equations of any degree of complexity we like, for

$$\mathbf{M}^{-1}(\mathbf{Mx}) = \mathbf{M}^{-1}\mathbf{a}$$
$$\mathbf{Ix} = \mathbf{M}^{-1}\mathbf{a}$$
$$\mathbf{x} = \mathbf{M}^{-1}\mathbf{a}$$

Though the theory is very elegant particularly when the number of simultaneous equations increases beyond two to 3, 4, 5 or more, the practical difficulty of finding $\mathbf{M}^{-1}$ can become rather tedious, though of course for a 2×2 matrix it is simple enough, especially if a modified matrix, rather than the actual inverse is used.

$$\begin{pmatrix} 7 & 8 \\ 6 & -5 \end{pmatrix} \begin{pmatrix} x \\ y \end{pmatrix} = \begin{pmatrix} 23 \\ -4 \end{pmatrix}$$

$$\begin{pmatrix} -5 & -8 \\ -6 & 7 \end{pmatrix} \begin{pmatrix} 7 & 8 \\ 6 & -5 \end{pmatrix} \begin{pmatrix} x \\ y \end{pmatrix} = \begin{pmatrix} -5 & -8 \\ -6 & 7 \end{pmatrix} \begin{pmatrix} 23 \\ -4 \end{pmatrix}$$

$$\begin{pmatrix} -83 & 0 \\ 0 & -83 \end{pmatrix} \begin{pmatrix} x \\ y \end{pmatrix} = \begin{pmatrix} -83 \\ -166 \end{pmatrix}$$

$$\begin{pmatrix} x \\ y \end{pmatrix} = \begin{pmatrix} 1 \\ 2 \end{pmatrix}$$

5. *Use of determinants*

If $\quad ax + by + c = 0$
and $dx + ey + f = 0$,

then
$$\frac{x}{\begin{vmatrix} b & c \\ e & f \end{vmatrix}} = \frac{-y}{\begin{vmatrix} a & c \\ d & f \end{vmatrix}} = \frac{1}{\begin{vmatrix} a & b \\ d & e \end{vmatrix}}$$

This is a fairly high-powered *result* which can be obtained in a variety of ways, but once *accepted* is clearly useful for subsequent calculation, so in our case.

$$\frac{x}{\begin{vmatrix} 8 & -23 \\ -5 & 4 \end{vmatrix}} = \frac{-y}{\begin{vmatrix} 7 & -23 \\ 6 & 4 \end{vmatrix}} = \frac{1}{\begin{vmatrix} 7 & 8 \\ 6 & -5 \end{vmatrix}}$$

or $\dfrac{x}{-83} = \dfrac{-y}{+166} = \dfrac{1}{-83}$

In particular if computer facilities exist, it is fairly straightforward to write a program to solve repeated pairs of simultaneous equations (Fig. 60). Print statements of course could be incorporated as required.

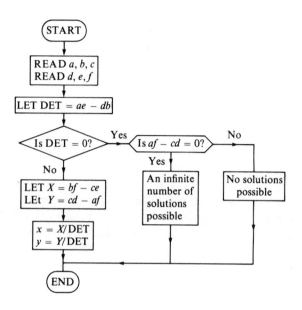

Fig. 60.

Pythagoras' Theorem
There are probably more proofs and demonstrations of this result than any other in the whole realm of mathematics. Out of the many here are a few. Quite an interesting exercise is to ask pupils to collect other demonstrations and proofs.

Euclid's proof
In essence this proof consists of showing that the square on the hypotenuse can be divided into two rectangles by means of a line drawn from *C* perpendicular to the hypotenuse *AB* and produced (see Fig. 61).

The areas of the two rectangles thus formed can be shown to be respectively equal to the squares on the other two sides.

95

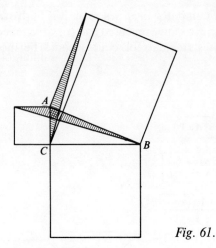

Fig. 61.

In the original demonstration this was done by considering first the two shaded triangles, and showing they were congruent by S.A.S. Then use was made of the theorem that the area of a rectangle on a given base and between two given parallels is twice that a triangle on the same base and between the same parallels. Similarly for the second rectangle. A more modern approach might use terms such as rotations and shears but fundamentally would be the same.

Using two squares of side $(a + b)$ (Fig. 62)

Square I   = Square II
Square I   = 4 triangles + c^2
Square II = 4 triangles + $a^2 + b^2$
Since the triangles are all congruent,
$$a^2 + b^2 = c^2$$

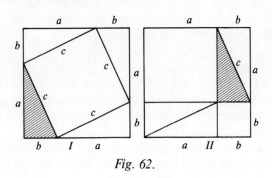

Fig. 62.

Perigal's dissection (Fig. 63)

From the centre of the 'middle sized' square draw lines parallel and perpendicular to the hypotenuse *AB*. This divides that squares into four equal parts which can be fitted together with the smallest square to make up the square on the hypotenuse.

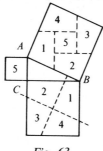

Fig. 63.

Trigonometrical proof (Fig. 64)

$$\cos A = \frac{b}{c} = \frac{x}{b} \Longrightarrow b^2 = xc$$

$$\cos B = \frac{a}{c} = \frac{y}{a} \Longrightarrow a^2 = yc$$

Adding: $a^2 + b^2 = (x + y)c = c^2$

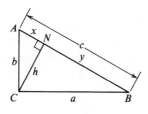

Fig. 64.

Trigonometry – sines, cosines, and tangents

The traditional approach is through an extension of work on right angled triangles and the *practical knowledge* that solutions to problems of the real world can often be obtained by the use of similar triangles. So, for example, a well known method of finding the height of a flag pole is to compare the length of the shadow of the pole with that of the shadow of a stick of known length when held vertically (see Fig. 65).

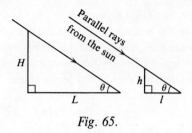

Fig. 65.

So $\dfrac{H}{h} = \dfrac{L}{l}$

$$H = \frac{h}{l} \cdot L$$

In this work the ratio, h/l, remains constant, and the height of various objects could all be obtained in the same way (provided their shadows were all measured at the same time). If further we observe that this ratio depends only on the angle the sun's rays make with the horizontal, θ as we are assuming that both triangles are right angled, we are led to consider the dependence of this ratio on the angle, and so to the traditional tangent function.

In the same way we can define the ratios for sine and cosine within the context of right angled triangles. This approach is still probably the best for those not going on to further mathematics, whose applications are likely to be of this very limited kind.

However, for those going on, other aspects are of far greater importance; the idea of periodicity, of wave motion, of the connection of sine and cosine with complex numbers, of applications in the calculus, and of approximating to any function by means of an infinite sum of sines and cosines.

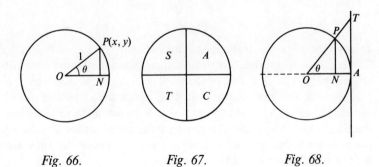

Fig. 66.   *Fig. 67.*   *Fig. 68.*

The traditional approach is modified by reference to the unit circle. In the first quadrant the co-ordinates of a point $P(x,y)$ where OP is 1 unit are shown to be equal to (cos θ, sin θ). Tan θ is then y/x or sin $\theta/\cos \theta$ (see Fig. 66). *These* definitions are now used to define the function in other quadrants and we get the familiar diagram which shows which functions are positive in which quadrants (Fig. 67). Since this is the later approach there are arguments for a change in the initial approach. Some of these are discussed below.

The unit circle approach (Fig. 68)
A point P moves in a circle of unit radius around a centre O, and with OP forming an angle θ with a fixed direction OA. The perpendicular from P meets OA (produced if necessary) at N, and OP (or PO) produced meets the tangent to the circle at A in the point T. The three functions are then defined as follows:

sin $\theta = PN$ (positive if P is above OA, negative if below)
cos $\theta = ON$ (positive if N is to the right of O, negative if to the left)
tan $\theta = TA$ (positive if T is above A, negative if below)

This certainly shows periodicity but is a trifle unnatural in that unit circles don't often occur and the similarities to applications in triangles have to be very carefully shown. However it does perhaps explain where the name *tangent* for this particular trigonometric function came from.

The displacements approach (Fig. 69)

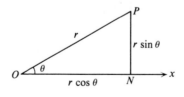

Fig. 69.

This is the approach followed by SMP and one is asked to think about the effective displacement in two directions at right angles – the *central* and *sideways* displacements of any vector OP. These two displacements are given by $r \cos \theta$, and $r \sin \theta$ respectively, and of course if $r = 1$ we are back at the unit circle. This approach has the merit of not defining the function in terms of right angled triangles and of using the same definition for angles of any size. By the use of the words *central* and *sideways*, there is of course a built in mnemonic to aid the memory.

Pattern and periodic change

This approach begins with considerations of patterns that recur in space (as seen in many forms of art); in time (phases of the moon, position of hands of the clock, dance figures, music); then patterns in space constructed to represent patterns in time such as time-tables, length of daylight graph, tide level graph, etc. and mental patterns (squares, mod 10: 0 1 4 9 6 5 6 9 4 1 0 1 4 9 . . . , cubes, mod 5: 0 1 3 2 4 0 . . . , recurring decimals). This leads to the idea of periodicity, and the naturalness of looking for such patterns. If a bicycle wheel is mounted horizontally and a vertical rod fastened to its rim and it is then spun, from sone distance away the apparent distance of the rod from the centre constantly recurs. In this approach, which is not too different from that of the unit circle, angles of *any magnitude* are met with right from the start.

Wrapping functions and radian measure

This approach has been developed to meet the increasing emphasis on the analytic properties of the trigonometric functions, and the need to have an interpretation of their properties quite apart from any direct reference to angles at all.

As an introduction, consider wrapping a length of string around a square, taking the length of string wrapped anti-clockwise from the origin as the independent variable, and the distance from the x-axis as the dependent variable in Fig. 70.

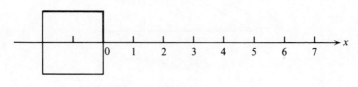

Fig. 70.

A physical model with a graph paper background for graphing and a square block of wood with twine wrapped round may make this more intelligible. The graph looks like Fig. 71.

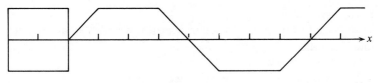

Fig. 71.

Wrapping functions for other shapes may now be considered (Fig. 72).

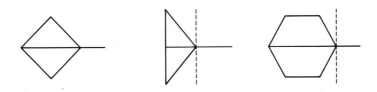

Fig. 72.

Consider now a wrapping of the *unit circle* (Fig. 73). Such a process established the ordered pair (cos x, sin x) where x is a real number as the co-ordinates of points on the unit circle. The complete 'trigonometry' of the functions can be developed without having to make any reference to angles at any point in the development. However, if at any time, it should be desirable to compare the circular functions of real numbers with the trigonometric functions of angles, the comparison can be effected through the medium of radian measure. The one to one correspondence which can thus be set up affords a simple method for the evaluation of the circular functions of real numbers.

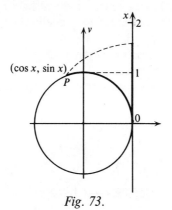

Fig. 73.

Logarithms

Traditionally the work on logarithms is developed in a sequence much as follows:

(1) Basic work with powers and indices

(2) Laws of operations with indices, in particular:

$$a^m \cdot a^n = a^{m+n}; \frac{a^m}{a^n} = a^{m-n};$$

$$a^0 = 1; (a^m)^n = a^{mn}; \sqrt[n]{a^m} = a^{\frac{m}{n}}.$$

(3) The comparison between adding natural numbers, and multiplying numbers expressed as powers, for example:

Natural number	0	1	2	3	4	5	6	7	8	9	10
Number in power form	2^0	2^1	2^2	2^3	2^4	2^5	2^6	2^7	2^8	2^9	2^{10}
Number		1	2	4	8	16	32	64	128	256	512	1024

$$8 \times 64 = 3^3 \times 2^6 = 2^9 = 512$$

(4) Giving meaning to powers like (0.5)

(5) Showing graphically the plausibility of expressing any number between 1 and 10 as a power of 10.

(6) Extending this to *any number* greater than one by use of the standard form $N = A \times 10^n$ where A lies between 1 and 10, and n is an integer.

(7) Reading tables of logarithms, and using them to express numbers as powers of ten:

    (i)   Numbers having two significant figures

    (ii) Numbers having three significant figures

    (iii) Numbers having four significant figures

(8) Practice with multiplication (results less than 10), writing numbers as powers, e.g. $3.27 = 10^{0.5145}$

(9) Practice with multiplication (results greater than 10) still writing numbers as powers.

(10) Dropping index form and writing logarithms as side work, e.g.

$$6.734 \times 8.205 = 55.29$$

Number	Log
6.734	0.8283
8.205	0.9143
55.29 ←	1.7426

(11) Logarithms of numbers less than one.

(12) Consolidation

Most of this work is so familiar as to need no comment, but at stage (11), the following may be of use. Consider the array of natural numbers in the accompanying figure. This array is characterised by the fact that in any *row* the *first* digit remains the same, and in any *column*, the last digit remains the same.

If we consider the process of repeated subtraction of ten from say 74, we get the sequence:

74, 64, 54, 44, 34, 24, 14, 4, − 6?! This seems a pity!

In the array the positions of − 10, − 20, − 30, etc. are obvious, but what of labels for the other points? If the pattern is to be maintained the final digit should remain constant and we are led to express − 6 as (− 10 + 4) and to indicate this by $\overline{1}4$.

90	91	92	93	94	95	96	97	98	99
80	81	82	83	84	85	86	87	88	89
70	71	72	73	74	75	76	77	78	79
60	61	62	63	64	65	66	67	68	69
50	51	52	53	54	55	56	57	58	59
40	41	42	43	44	45	46	47	48	49
30	31	32	33	34	35	36	37	38	39
20	21	22	23	24	25	26	27	28	29
10	11	12	13	14	15	16	17	18	19
0	1	2	3	4	5	6	7	8	9
− 10	·	·	·	$\overline{1}4$	·	·	·	·	·
− 20	·	·	·	$\overline{2}4$	·	·	·	·	·
− 30	·	·	·	$\overline{3}4$	·	·	·	·	·

Somewhat similar considerations in logarithms make us want to associate a certain definite unchanged sequence of numbers in the *logarithm* for any given sequence of significant figures.

So for   3425, the logarithm is 3.*5346*   or 3 + 0.5346
for   342.5, the logarithm is 2.*5346*   2 + 0.5346
for   34.25, the logarithm is 1.*5346*   1 + 0.5346
for   3.425, the logarithm is 0.*5346*   0 + 0.5346
for 0.3425, the logarithm is ?.*5346*   −1 + 0.5346

Finding what to put in place of the question mark should now present no difficulty.

Growth functions

Some developments stress the idea of functions and their inverses. So if we regard a mapping (function) of the type $x \longrightarrow a^x$ as a growth function, we are led to consider the inverse mapping $a^x \longrightarrow x$, which is more commonly known as the logarithmic function, $x = \log_a(a^x)$. Put another way, $x = \log_a M \Longleftrightarrow M = a^x$.

This function has the characteristic that if M and N are numbers and $x = \log_a M$ and $y = \log_a N$, then $z = \log_a(MN) = x + y$. Let us look then for functions with this characteristic and in particular consider $f : x \longrightarrow 1/x$.

Let us define a function $A(x)$ as the area under this curve from 1 to x. Thus $A(1) = 0$, and $A(3)$ is shaded in Fig. 74.

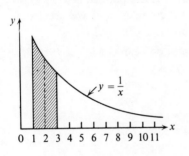

Fig. 74.   *Fig. 75.*

Consider the transformation of this region by the matrix $\begin{pmatrix} 4 & 0 \\ 0 & \frac{1}{4} \end{pmatrix}$.

Then the points $(1, 0), (1, 1), (2, 0), (2, \frac{1}{2}), (3, 0), (3, \frac{1}{3})$ are transformed into $(4, 0), (4, \frac{1}{4}), (8, 0), (8, \frac{1}{8}), (12, 0), (12, \frac{1}{12})$ respectively.

So $A(3) \longrightarrow A(12) - A(4)$ and since the area factor of the transformation in *one*, we have $A(3) = A(12) - A(4)$

$$\text{or } A(3) + A(4) = A(12) \text{ (see Fig. 75)}.$$

The area function $A(x)$ therefore behaves like a logarithmic function. The only thing left unspecified is the base to which the logarithms apply.

These examples from the multiplication of directed numbers, simultaneous linear equations, Pythagoras' theorem, trigonometry, and the teaching of logarithms have been given to illustrate that the mathematics itself can be approached in different ways and that when this is put alongside the need for catering for individual differences, and for recognising the different stages in the learning process, there is laid upon us as teachers the constant necessity for ensuring variety so as to give meaning and vitality to our teaching.

The Instructional file

If any of the ideas above are new to readers they should suggest the need for keeping an instructional file. This file is best kept in a loose leaf binder, and its purpose is to keep on record valuable ideas which may subsequently be useful and which, if not recorded, may easily be forgotten. It will include ideas for introductions to lessons, alternative strategies or approaches, illuminating examples, possible starting points for investigations, puzzles, paradoxes, problems. Entries need not be long, but they will be made much more useful if they are given a heading and filed in alphabetical order for ease of reference. Possible entries might be those shown in Figs. 76, 77.

Fig. 76.

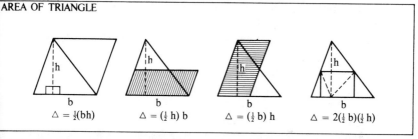

AREA OF TRIANGLE

$\triangle = \frac{1}{2}(bh)$ $\triangle = (\frac{1}{2} h) b$ $\triangle = (\frac{1}{2} b) h$ $\triangle = 2(\frac{1}{2} b)(\frac{1}{2} h)$

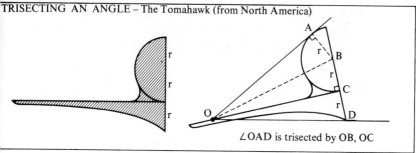

TRISECTING AN ANGLE – The Tomahawk (from North America)

∠OAD is trisected by OB, OC

Fig. 77.

Sources for ideas are conferences, lectures, books, professional magazines, but best of all discussions with fellow teachers.

Summary

Let us summarise below the principles of strategy outlined above.

(1) Don't tell students any result they can *reasonably* discover directly or be led to discover by suitably framed questions or work sheets. Compare for example the difference of attitude engendered by the two questions:

(i) "Prove that the inscribed angle is half that at the centre," and (ii) "Is there a relationship between the inscribed angle and the angle at the centre, and if so, what is it?"

(2) Ensure variety. This includes the provision of definite sessions for creative work, problem solving, and practical work as well as variety of approach in the mathematics itself.

(3) In concept formation, put things before words, concrete before abstract, doing and seeing before verbal expression. Learning begins with action and perception, proceeds from thence to words and concepts and should end in desirable mental habits.

(4) In developing skills, apply the following principles of practice. Set work that:

can be done with intent to improve;

can be done thoughtfully;

follows discovery and understanding (it is reinforced understanding that is important);

involves correct responses (this is more important than speed);

is individualised, i.e. altered according to the student's ability;

is brief and at spaced intervals;

is given in meaningful exercises;

emphasises general principles, e.g. the associative and distributive laws.

There should be a variety of activities, games, contests, puzzles, timed exercises, mental computation, group activities, oral or written exercises. The learner should be *kept informed* of his progress. Practice should never be given as a punishment.

(5) Grade work according to the needs and abilities of students.

(6) Expect students to memorise only those results they *frequently* use.

(7) Plan carefully the stages in progress that each student must pass through.

(8) Provide yourself with an 'instructional file' in which to keep a record of ideas which you have found stimulating, and which may be of use to you in your own teaching.

6. Method

We come now to the crux of teaching where theory is translated into practice. In this chapter we are going to discuss different types of lessons and give some bases for decision as to which type of lesson is most appropriate in various circumstances. We shall find in particular very close connections with both strategy and materials, though naturally the whole of the teaching process outlined in the first chapter will be constantly in our minds.

Scheme of work

The starting point in practical terms is a 'Scheme of Work' outlining the content that it is hoped will be covered during the course of the year. Within this we shall have to break down the work into smaller units, to define the topics we hope to cover within a term, at least with the majority of the class. In determining this content we must bear in mind how the topics chosen relate to the rest of the academic programme, what has gone before and to what further developments the new competence and understanding leads. We will need to consider what teaching techniques are to be used, particularly any that require long term planning. The sort of consideration here is the use of a television or broadcast series, the acquiring of the necessary teacher's and pupils' notes and possibly workbooks, and arranging rooms and time-tables to accommodate these plans; the ordering of films from outside agencies. We need also to think about how the programme we are embarking upon is to be evaluated, and whether for example, pre-testing at the beginning of the term is appropriate, or whether it would kill any hope of a satisfactory relationship being set up between ourselves and our pupils. In some schools this long term planning is done by the Head of Department himself or in joint consultation with the whole mathematics department. Such consultation can be of immense benefit to all concerned, for it is most likely that the students you have one year will be taught by someone else the following year, and if there is a common policy and commonly defined objectives and approaches, the transition for the student is likely to be much easier, and the work of the department more efficient.

Unit plans

Unit planning is the intermediate stage between the termly *Scheme of Work* and the *Daily Lesson Plan*. Its purpose is to put the daily lessons into broader perspective and at the same time force a deeper analysis of the content to be taught. It also means that if progress is surprisingly quick, the teacher is prepared for the next step and is not caught out with insufficient material prepared. Here are some of the questions that should be considered in organising plans for a substantial segment of work:

(1) Why is this unit important? What is its place in the overall content of the course? What does it have in it that is likely to appeal to students? What are the keys to future progress?

(2) What are the central ideas and unifying concepts around which activities may be organised? What should be stressed most? How long will this work take, and how should the time be subdivided?

(3) What teaching strategies are appropriate? Is this the first time students have met these ideas, or is it a question of giving wider perspectives to ideas previously introduced? Can students discover the basic concepts themselves? What materials are available to provide a varied attack on the unit?

(4) What preliminary concepts, skills and experiences are needed as background for this unit? How can the content be modified for students of varying ability? What extra practice can be provided for weak students? What special teaching techniques may be used with them? What can other students do when weaker students receive special attention? What enrichment topics should be included for all students? What provision can be made for the very bright?

(5) What teaching techniques will best suit this class? What are the points of special difficulty? How did I teach this material previously? Should I change my approach or techniques? Is there an opportunity for practical work?

(6) What materials will this unit require? What supplementary books or pamphlets would be helpful for students? What models, films, or other visual aids are appropriate? What should the bulletin board display? Are any field trips or excursions suitable? Who might be a suitable outside speaker or class participant?

(7) What kind of evaluation should I use? What ways are best suited to the content of this unit and to this class? Should I pre-test?

(8) What kinds of work should be given for students to do on their own? Is there a place for a long-term assignment? Can the students learn part of the material independently?

These questions help to pin down amorphous thinking about teaching problems and help the teacher escape from the textbook. They provide the basis of careful development that will be put into practice by the daily lesson plans and classroom procedures.

The daily Lesson Plan

Well-planned lessons give confidence to the teacher which in turn rubs off on the class. They ensure that there is both progress and continuity. Their format may vary but in their preparation the teacher should answer much the same questions as in the unit plan but now on the time scale of a single lesson, whether a single or a double period. The list that follows tries to be fairly comprehensive, but it may seem too daunting a list for regular use by a hard-pressed teacher. If this is so, it can be compressed into three basic questions, 'What?', 'Why?', and 'How?'. However, in their expanded form the questions are as follows:

(1) What am I going to teach? Or what experiences am I going to arrange for the students?

(2) Why is it important for students to learn these ideas or have these experiences?

(3) Is an introduction appropriate, and if so what form should it take?

(4) How is the body of the lesson going to be built up? What key questions should I ask? How can I ensure that students discover things for themselves?

(5) What materials will I need?

(6) What kinds of learning activity are appropriate? In particular do I need work cards? If so, have I enough and of sufficient variety?

(7) How am I going to end the lesson? What arrangements are necessary for setting work or collecting it in?

At the conclusion of the lesson, the teacher should ask himself:

(i) Did I achieve my objective? If not, why not?

(ii) What points from this lesson must I bear in mind in preparing my next lesson?

(iii) Did anything occur in this lesson which is worth remembering for future reference?

The lesson plan may have any convenient format and may vary in thoroughness, but if a lesson has not been properly prepared and planned, it is rarely a success, and the subsequent evaluation may be rather disconcerting!

In answering the basic questions, 'Why?' and 'What?' we need to bear in mind some of the varied objectives that specific lessons may have. These may include one or more of the following:

To provide initial experience in a new field on which concepts may later be built;

To gather information, statistics, or make models which will be used in subsequent lessons;

To introduce a new topic, concept, or skill;

To apply newly acquired skills in concrete situations;

To maintain a skill by adequate provision of practice;

To consolidate ideas gained in previous lessons;

To review a section of work;

To give practice in 'translating' problems expressed in English into the language of mathematics;

To develop students' ability to express mathematical ideas coherently and effectively;

To engender independent enquiry, and foster creative mathematical thought;

To assess students' attainment, and evaluate the effectiveness of the teaching they have received.

Types of Lesson

Let us now look at a variety of different types of lesson that are available to us so that with our objective defined we can choose which of them singly or which combination of them is most appropriate to our immediate requirements. Lessons may be broadly divided into three main kinds:

Full class lessons

These are lessons in which the whole class is engaged in the same activity at the same time. Frequently this is the only kind of lesson one sees in secondary schools, and this in spite of the acknowledged differences that exist in pupils both as to aptitude and interest. However, even in 'modern' teaching there are many occasions when full class participation is the most efficient form of organisation.

Group lessons

In these lessons the class is divided into groups, and each group is given something specific to do. Often the specific assignments for each group may be quite different. This may be entirely to cater for differences of ability when it is normally referred to as ability grouping; or because of limitations of equipment; or as a means of getting quickly a variety of information, statistics, or models that will subsequently be used by the whole class. It is possible to arrange that some of the better students can help conduct these small groups. As they do so they will learn mathematics, learn to communicate, and gain experience in a leadership role.

Individualised lessons

These are lessons in which assignments are normally set on work cards or by the use of programmed texts. In this case students work on their own, or in pairs at their own rate. This certainly caters for individual differences, but loses out on the social aspects of education which are much more strongly stressed in the group lessons, and even in full class lessons.

Among the types of lessons which can be conducted with a whole class are the following:

Broadcast lessons

These may be based on either television or radio broadcasts. In either case a good deal of help is given to the teacher in the form of printed notes that outline the substance of the material to be broadcast and frequently in addition give suggestions for follow-up work and sometimes even pupils' booklets in which such follow-up work can be done. It is essential if a broadcast is to form part of a lesson, that it is seen to be an integral part of it. In particular the teacher must watch his timing, see that an appropriate introduction is given beforehand and that there is time for discussion and comment afterwards. This is one type of lesson that needs long term preparation, in particular the ordering of the appropriate notes; for without knowing either the content or approach of any broadcast before it is given, the teacher is bound to lose much of the effectiveness of the expertise that is incorporated in the broadcast itself.

Films

A film can often serve a very useful purpose, either as an introduction to a topic; or as a suitable focus for discussion at the conclusion of a section of work. Again if it is to be most effectively used, the teacher should have seen the film previously and considered any comments he may wish to insert as it progresses as well as prepare specific questions to ask at its conclusion.

Short films and film loops, film strips and other audio-visual aids can be used also in the development of a topic, in trying to provide a

111

new stimulus or motivation for students; and can form an integral part of a programme of either group or individual instruction as well as being used with a whole class.

Games

There are many games now available commercially and others that can be prepared by students that can promote the learning of mathematics in an interesting and entertaining way. The judicious use of competitions can also be an aid to practising mechanical skills. Verbal presentations can also form a useful introduction to a lesson, for example the game, 'What number?' The leader thinks of a rule, say 'Subtract 2' and invites various members of the class to give him numbers at random. Given 17 he replies 15; given 13 he replies 11, and so on until someone indicates that he thinks he knows the rule. The leader then gives this person a number and if the response is correct, says 'Right – what then is the rule?' The person who discovered it replies and then becomes the leader for the next round.

Visiting speakers

The visit of an outside speaker often gives to a course a flavour and importance that is different, yet stimulating. It implies the search by the teacher of an authority on the subject to come specially for *his class*, and this can have great repercussions on motivation and on student–teacher relationships. A talk by an outside speaker can often be the starting point for individual and group investigations in all sorts of directions, and so be a stimulus to mathematical activity and growth.

Field trips (education visits)

As with the case of visiting speakers field trips can be a way of providing vivid learning experiences which add realism and pleasure to mathematics lessons. They often result in better learning than other forms of educational experience because we usually recall travel experiences much more accurately and intensively than classroom learning experiences. A carefully planned field trip is particularly well suited to attain such goals as the following:

(1) To provide *motivation* for the study of a unit.

(2) To enrich mathematical learnings by relating school work to actual life situations.

(3) To provide specific materials for later use in class.

112

(4) To generate realistic situations for group planning and thus fulfil a social role.

(5) To present material in a natural setting.

(6) To integrate the subject matter of different courses.

(7) To provide a means for many students and community citizens to participate in the school programme.

Suitable places to visit are government agencies, such as the post office, weather bureau, road development headquarters; community institutions like museums, art centres, churches; business enterprises like factories, banks, engineering offices, supermarkets; transportation centres such as the airport, bus depot, freight office; public utilities such as the telephone centre, electric or gas companies, water plant.

The success of such visits depends on careful planning. Successful planning involves selecting an appropriate trip, making the necessary arrangements, arranging for supervision on the visit, and providing suitable follow-up activities. It is important that the teacher should help students to identify or discover the mathematical aspects of what they see, and that these aspects should be tied in with what has been learned in class.

Consider for example a visit to a bank. The teacher's part would be to provide a guide sheet. This might include the following:

(1) A flow chart of how a cheque is processed.

(2) A question concerning the use of calculators and computers.

(3) Illustrations of interest tables and comparisons of different types of investment.

(4) A question about what is required of a customer to establish credit facilities.

(5) Questions about employment opportunities and necessary qualifications. Without some such guide sheet the mathematics could well be overlooked.

Introducing a new topic

Much of what has been said so far may seem to represent fringe activities, which while adding variety and interest, don't bear greatly on the main work of the course which is concerned with introducing new concepts, consolidating these concepts, setting up a maintenance schedule for skills, and ensuring thorough and complete revision. These aspects of course work are constantly with us whether we use a full class, group methods, or individualised instruction and there are basic principles that are common to all.

113

The first is the idea of trying as far as possible to make children 'discover' the new concepts or processes for themselves. The implication of this is to avoid telling children results when the results can be obtained indirectly either through a well thought out sequence of question and answer, or by organising work in such a way that results are put side by side so as to invite conjecture. Some excellent examples of this technique are found in the book, *Some lessons in mathematics*, edited by T. J. Fletcher and published by C.U.P. Here a variety of 'new' topics are introduced by skilful questioning, or by the posing of open problems, or by activities which result in a record in which a pattern is noticed. This pattern in turn leads to a conjecture which subsequently can be shown to be either true or false. The point is that such a process involves children in *doing mathematics*, in making their approach *active* rather than passive, and thus of making more likely a strong motivation for the subsequent work of practice and consolidation.

The second principle is when introducing an idea which involves a relationship to give a lot of examples with simple numerical terms so that the *relationship* is stressed, not the arithmetical computation. For example, consider this outline lesson for finding the area of a circle (see Fig. 78).

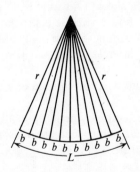

Fig. 78.

First get each child to draw a sector of a circle and divide it up into 'thin triangles' and then to draw in 'straight bases'. It will be seen that the arc of the circle corresponds very closely to a succession of short straight lines. Then by suitable questioning establish that if this sector is divided into n triangles each of base b, the area of each triangle is $\frac{1}{2}rb$. The total area of the sector is then $n(\frac{1}{2}rb)$. (Note: For some students, actual *numbers* will have to be used instead of the algebraic generality implied here.) We may now write:

$$\text{Area of sector} = n(\tfrac{1}{2}rb) = \tfrac{1}{2}r(nb) \text{ using Associative law}$$
$$= \tfrac{1}{2}rL \text{ (where } L \text{ is the length of the arc)}$$

At this stage give six or seven quick calculations in which values of r and L are given so that the relationship is immediately applied, and confidence is gained in getting right results, e.g.: $r = 2, L = 3; r = 6, L = 8; r = 4, L = 5; r = 5, L = 6$; etc.

Now for a given value of r, say 7, gradually increase L (still using simple values) until eventually $L = C$, the circumference of the circle (Fig. 79).

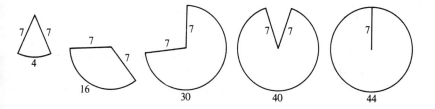

Fig. 79.

Then Area of Circle $= \tfrac{1}{2}rC$
$$\text{But} \qquad C = 2\pi r \qquad \text{(result from previous work)}$$
So Area of circle $= \tfrac{1}{2}r\,(2\pi r)$
$$= \pi r^2$$

Again use this result immediately taking $\pi = \tfrac{22}{7}$ and $r = 1, 2, 7, 14$; and then $\pi = 3.14$ and $r = 10, 20, 5$. Only then should we use more difficult values for r, when the stress moves from *understanding* the relation to *using it* in more realistic situations.

A third principle is that if the teacher decides to use the same approach to a topic as that in the text, he should *not* use precisely the same numerical values as the example in the text. The point is that any student following the teacher's explanation, and then the example in the book will have *twice* as much background experience as he would have done if the *same* example were used. Essential similarities will become apparent, while differences will be noted. Abstraction of principles comes from a variety of experience. If there is only one example, abstraction is virtually impossible.

115

Consolidation

After a topic has been introduced there must be a period of consolidation. This implies students doing examples on their own employing the new technique or principle. These lessons are perhaps the least exciting to outside observers, but they are absolutely essential. The standard lesson is an introduction consisting of a quick review of previous work and some comment on the need for practice, accuracy, and speed, and then the setting of further examples. At this stage, of course, some account must be taken of individual differences, by setting questions of varying degrees of difficulty and by the introduction of work cards either of a remedial nature for the weaker students, or of further examples of the same standard for the average, or of a more challenging variety for the bright (see p. 75). While students are working, the teacher should be going round the class, helping where necessary, and marking as correct examples properly done. This gives satisfaction and confidence to the student and cuts down on marking time when work is handed in.

In the case of skills, consolidation implies the setting up of a maintenance schedule. This involves selecting the skills to be maintained; then ensuring that practice is not too concentrated but recurs at increasing intervals and in decreasing amounts. The implication of this is that after a first introduction, the consolidation of a particular skill will rarely occupy a full lesson; rather there will be times within lessons devoted to this purpose. Suitable provision for this must be made in unit and daily lesson plans. Any practice ideally should incorporate diagnostic, and if possible self-diagnostic, features. Two special features may be of interest:

The first of these is the 'domino' technique in which a number of cards are made which are divided into two parts, one of which is a question, the other an answer. The idea is to pick up *any* card, read the question part of that card, find the answer on another card and put it alongside (like matching dominoes). This then provides a second question and so on (see Fig. 80). The last question (the nth)

Answer n	Question 1		Answer 1	Question 2		Answer 2	Question 3	

Fig. 80.

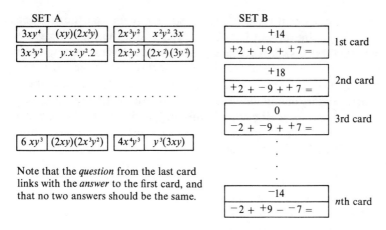

SET A

$3xy^4$	$(xy)(2x^2y)$	$2x^3y^2$	$x^2y^2.3x$
$3x^3y^2$	$y.x^2.y^2.2$	$2x^2y^3$	$(2x^2)(3y^2)$

. . . .

$6\,xy^3$	$(2xy)(2x^3y^2)$	$4x^4y^3$	$y^3(3xy)$

Note that the *question* from the last card links with the *answer* to the first card, and that no two answers should be the same.

SET B

$^{+}14$	1st card
$^{+}2 + \,^{+}9 + \,^{+}7 =$	

$^{+}18$	2nd card
$^{+}2 + \,^{-}9 + \,^{+}7 =$	

0	3rd card
$^{-}2 + \,^{-}9 + \,^{+}7 =$	

.

.

.

$^{-}14$	nth card
$^{-}2 + \,^{+}9 - \,^{-}7 =$	

In this set, cards are divided horizontally instead of vertically

Fig. 81.

should have as its answer the answer part on the *first* domino. If this is not so, then there is a mistake. The material is thus self-correcting.

Two examples of possible sets of cards are given in Fig. 81. If the cards are used regularly, students can time themselves to see how long it takes them to set out all the cards, and then try to improve on their time. A graph of times taken can be made if desired, and kept by the individual student.

Another technique useful for pairs of students is the flash card technique. Cards are produced with questions on one side, answers on the other (see Fig. 82). Students work in pairs. The cards are

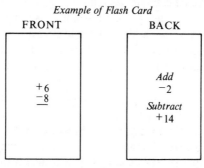

Example of Flash Card

FRONT   BACK

$^{+}6$
$^{-}8$

Add
$^{-}2$
Subtract
$^{+}14$

Fig. 82.

117

shuffled and one student acts as questioner by showing the questions in turn to the other. The other replies and the first one knows whether the answer is correct or not as the answer is written on the side facing him. When they have gone through all the cards, they are shuffled, and the roles of questioner and responder are changed.

Elementary manipulative skills of both arithmetic and algebra can be practised most efficiently in this way, and remedial work can be done without interrupting the rest of the class. There is the added psychological advantage that there is no *record* of mistakes!

Revision lessons

From time to time it is necessary to review work and refresh memories so that material once learned is not forgotten, and so that links are consciously made between different aspects of work which previously may have seemed unrelated. Both these aspects of revision are important. The first, of keeping work fresh in mind, implies that review lessons should occur more frequently than perhaps they do, and certainly more often than once a term or once a year! Many of the better textbooks make provision for this in their very structure. The second, of consciously making links, is most important in the mathematical education of students. At the start of any course only the teacher really understands the interrelation of all the topics that are included. By the end, every students should do so as well. Very often review is made more effective if a different strategy or approach is used from that in the initial introduction so that the material, while not *new*, is still fresh. This again lays on the teacher the obligation to search constantly for new strategies and approaches.

Student directed class discussion

As a change from teacher presentation it is useful periodically (and especially during revision time) to ask students to lead the class through some aspect of the work. Student participation can also be encouraged by asking them to make reports on individual or group projects, to show models they have made, and by some to report on enrichment material that they have been set individually. There are, in fact, many wonderful and exciting mathematical ideas for discussion that are not in the regular textbooks–topics such as historical incidents, applications, space travel, game theory. There is an increasing number of books with suggestions for this type of work on which we should capitalise.

Practical lessons

Although it is sometimes right to run practical lessons as whole class lessons, it is usually much more natural to divide the class into a number of groups. In the simplest cases when the number of groups is fairly small, say three or four, the assignments for each group can be given verbally; but usually it is more effective and more useful to issue *group work cards*. This is so because firstly it ensures that instructions are *explicit*, and secondly because it prepares the way for a much more radical procedure – the issue of *individual work cards*.

A typical situation where six to eight groups are desirable will be one involving *measurement* where the amount of apparatus available is limited and yet it is important that everyone should have a chance to see, handle, and use a variety of equipment. For example, in a series of lessons on metric measure we wish to give students experience with metric units of length, area, volume, and weight. We have available the following:

3 tape measures of 50 metres
2 balances with sets of weights up to 1 kilogramme
1 set of metric scales (bathroom scales)
Measuring cylinders marked in millilitres
1 micrometer screw gauge
2 calipers
Metric graph paper

We might then design a set of cards:

A1, 2, and 3 involving the measurement of objects, e.g. buildings, requiring the use of the tape measures.

B1, and 2, involving weighing a variety of specified objects.

C involving weighing every member of the group in kilogrammes and finding the average weight of the group.

D1, 2, and 3 involving volume, either direct capacity of various tins, etc. or indirectly using displacement.

E using the micrometer screw gauge.

F1 and 2 involving the use of calipers – perhaps associating this with an investigation into diameters and circumferences of various circular objects; or of distances between places on maps.

Each card will state:

(1) What equipment is required
(2) What measuring is to be done
(3) The form of any record required
(4) Whether any graph work, or calculation, is required.

```
              METRIC MEASUREMENTS
                    CARD A 1
              (DO NOT WRITE ON THIS CARD)
You will need: 50 metre tape measure, centimetre graph
paper
What to do:
   (1) Measure the length and breadth of the classroom
       in metres (to the nearest centimetre)
   (2) Record your results in your exercise book like this:
       CARD A 1    Length of classroom =        metres
                   Breadth of classroom =       metres
   (3) Make a scale drawing of the classroom floor using
       a scale of 1 cm to represent 1 metre.
   (4) What is the area of your scale drawing in square
       centimetres?
       What is the area of the classroom floor in square
       metres?
```

Fig. 83.

An example of such a card is given in Fig. 83.

It will be noted that there are about one and a half times as many cards required as groups, and that the primary objective is that *every* group should, in the course of a series of lessons, have an opportunity of using each type of apparatus A, B, C, D, E, and F, but will have to repeat *some* of these.

The teacher will prepare a matrix as follows:

METRIC MEASURE ASSIGNMENTS

	A1	A2	A3	B1	B2	C	D1	D2	D3	E	F1	F2
Group I	✓											
Group II			✓									
Group III				✓								
Group IV					✓							
Group V							✓					
Group VI										✓		

To begin with cards may be issued to groups as indicated by the ticks with the instruction that when the work outlined on the card has been completed and the necessary recording done in *individual* exercise books, both books and cards should be returned to the teacher.

Suppose Group II finishes first and brings in their work. They can then be assigned, say D2, and a stroke put across the tick ($\check{\times}$) under B1 to indicate that that particular assignment has been completed. In this way all groups are kept busy all the time, but the more able groups will complete more assignments over a period of time. Moreover the teacher will be able to give assistance where it is required most (probably on the micrometer screw gauge!). In due course all groups will be able to use all six types of equipment.

It might be noted that the results from C could later be brought together to find the average weight of the whole class. This might result in two different situations: (i) that where each group has the same number of children, or (ii) that in which some groups have different numbers of children. The second case would give rise to ideas of *weighted means*, while the first could be regarded as *samples* to approximate to the mean of the whole population (i.e. the whole class).

Problem solving

One aspect of problem solving (that of problems which require independent and often original thought) arises naturally from the investigation. For many students, however, problem solving has a very different connotation. *Problems* are contrasted in their minds with *manipulative skills*. They are questions which are stated in words rather than in mathematical symbols, and the biggest source of difficulty here is one of *language*; of translating the original statements of English into the corresponding statements of mathematics. It is useful therefore, from time to time, to have 'translation sessions', to set out just to write down appropriate equations and leave the solution to some other time. This is particularly so if we have a computer available, either actually or at least conceptually, which has a program 'to solve equations' but can't itself 'write equations'. The part of the mathematician is clearly to interpret the data and write the equations.

The Communication lesson

If 'translating' is one aspect of language in mathematics, there are others. For example many students lack skill in listening, reading, and studying. This means that we must teach these skills for they are essential for the independent learning of mathematics. So we must give prominence to the student's participation in class discussion. While one student is speaking, the others must be encouraged to pay attention to what is being said and to try to correct or improve upon statements made, to question statements that are not clear, to anticipate the line of argument a speaker is following, and to reflect upon what has been discussed in and out of class.

The individual student must also be made aware of the uniqueness of mathematical statements, their specialised vocabulary, the power of mathematical symbolism, the preciseness and conciseness of various definitions, the mathematical use of common words such as *set*, *group*, *root*, *base*, *irrational*, *real*. He should realise too our frequent dependence on Latin and Greek stems. Wherever possible these stems should be commented upon, e.g. *poly*gon, *poly*hedra, and this related to non-mathematical usage such as *poly*gamy; likewise *bi*nomial, *bi*monthly, *bi*sect, *bi*cycle. It is only by our being deliberately aware of this as an objective that we can help to build word mastery, for this grows in the following way: first words are heard with comprehension, then they are read, then used in speaking, and only finally in writing. If we try to get students to write precise statements before they have mastered the associated ideas or expressed them clearly verbally, their learning may well be hampered.

Classroom organisation

Having reviewed the possibilities as to the type or types of lesson we may employ we need to look into a number of points of organisation very briefly.

The first of these is that a number of the types of lesson we have outlined – practical work, investigations, experiments, work in groups, individual assignments, really require longer periods of time consecutively than the usual 40–45 minutes. As these activities are the ones through which it is hoped the overall objectives of *attitude* and *personal and social development* will be achieved, it seems desirable to try to build into the framework of the time-table at least one double period a week.

The second is that it is a wise principle of classroom organisation to set up procedures to carry out efficiently often repeated actions. Of these the collection and return of student's work is the most important. What the procedure is, is relatively unimportant so long as it is quick, efficient and quiet. I have found it useful to require students to leave their exercise books open at the page where new work has begun; in formal classes (in rows) to require the student at the back of each row to collect all the books in his row; in informal groups a nominated person in each group. When looking at the work for grading, correcting, or assessing, I kept the books in the same piles so that they could be returned with the minimum of fuss and time lost. A few minutes saved each day in this way amounts to a considerable saving of time over a whole year. In the same way procedures should be set up for the issue and return of equipment, this procedure having built into it a *count* of articles issued and returned!

Summary

Overall schemes of work, intermediate unit plans, and daily lesson plans, all follow the same basic outline as that followed by this book: aims and objectives, content, strategy, method, materials, and evaluation. Methods must be varied according to the needs and abilities of the students, the stages of learning, and the mathematics to be taught. A good programme of instruction will contain some lessons given to the whole class, others involving groups of students, and still others that are based on individual needs and abilities. Provision should be made for at least one double period a week to incorporate certain types of lesson which are desirable and which need this prolonged time allocation. Procedures should be established for the collection and return of student's work, the collection and return of equipment, and any other often repeated process so that unnecessary time is not spent on non-essentials.

123

7. Materials

Very closely connected with considerations of strategy and method are those connected with the type and availability of materials. In many cases, in fact, certain strategies and methods are precluded if the necessary materials are not available; in other cases the *limitation* of materials impose a group structure on lesson plans (see p. 119). Sometimes on the other hand the *availability* of certain resources encourage the teacher to experiment and try certain approaches that he would not perhaps otherwise have considered.

Of all the material resources commonly on hand by far the most common and most important is the textbook or textbook series in use in a school. In fact in many cases, this *aid* becomes the controlling influence or the determining factor for content, strategy, and approach! This is clearly undesirable, because no single book, or series of books can hope to meet the particular situations in a vast variety of schools with different kinds of pupils with different backgrounds, hopes, and aspirations. In fact it would appear that the ideal situation is to leave the planning and development for course work for any particular class in the hands of a competent class teacher. This implies for the teacher, however, considerable skill, a good and thorough knowledge of mathematics together with a sympathy towards and understanding of, student problems and capabilities. Most of all it implies *time*, time to plan, time to prepare visual aids, time to consider different strategies and methods, time to devote himself whole-heartedly to the particular class which has been entrusted to him. In practice this rarely, if ever, is the case, though of course good teachers *make* time to do all these things for each class periodically.

It is also often the case that the teacher's own background is limited, either in the field of mathematics itself, or in experience in dealing with groups of children of varying aptitudes and interests, or both. For such teachers, the textbook provides something of a prop, giving the requisite mathematical content, at least suggesting one or more approaches to presentation, and providing the necessary material for students to be involved in *doing* mathematics for themselves. It can therefore be a valuable resource, and in some cases is the *only* resource available to a teacher.

What then should we expect from a textbook? A good textbook will do the following things:

(a) Provide *most* of the content. A choice of supplementary material must be left to the teacher, this choice being dependent on the abilities and interests of the students concerned. This is often done by a series of supplementary *Topic* books.

(b) Present topics in a manner that builds understanding. In this respect one uses the expertise and experience of the writer or writers which often is very considerable.

(c) Provide exercises, experiences, directions for attaining mastery through practice, review, application and thought-provoking questions.

(d) Provide a means of independent study.

(e) Make provision for individual differences.

(f) Act as a compact reference book.

(g) Provide a basis for achievement testing.

In short a good textbook provides a *basis* for classroom instruction, a sort of launching pad from which the class may take off for further work or exploration either corporately under the guidance of the teacher, or individually when particular interests are aroused. It should *not* be regarded, however, as providing the complete and final answer to the whole course of instruction for any class.

Apart from textbooks there are now available a great number and variety of audio-visual aids. Some of these are listed below with comments as to their use. Very few schools will possess all or even most of these, but they are included for the sake of completeness.

(1) *Motion picture films*

A great number of mathematical films are now available. In many parts of the world libraries of films are kept by local education authorities or are obtainable on hire from a number of commercial firms. Reviews of films are made from time to time in various mathematical journals so that teachers can be kept informed of current supplies.

Films are particularly useful in presenting topics from the history of mathematics and other enrichment topics, in presenting ideas that depend on motion, for example ideas of locus and transformation geometry, and in helping correlate mathematics with other subjects. Sometimes a film is very useful as an introduction to a new subject or unit; on other occasions it may seem more appropriate to use it as a review unit at the conclusion of a course. Films also enable one to see important first hand accounts of new activities in mathematics, experimental approaches tried in various settings and so can serve a useful purpose in professional gatherings of teachers and in teacher training establishments. Lastly they can be used just as sheer delight, as for example the mini-films *Notes on a triangle* and *Dance squared*.

(2) *Filmstrips*

Filmstrips have several important advantages – they are inexpensive, any frame can be kept in view for as long as discussion is appropriate, and where necessary steps can be retraced. Even more flexible is the use of individually prepared slides by a teacher; and the making of such slides can form a useful project for a mathematics club.

(3) *Television*

This is a medium which is becoming increasingly important. Many television programme include topics in modern mathematics presented in a lively and entertaining way by experts. Frequently notes for teachers are available outlining what is going to be shown and suggesting activities for follow-up and discussion. These can be particularly useful for teachers who are not too confident about certain work, but who can with guidance, assimilate and pass on these topics to the children in their classes. The chief difficulty is to *incorporate* television lessons into the overall structure or schema of the course. However, many programmes also incorporate preview sessions, and are repeated in subsequent years. In this way teachers can become familiar with the material and approach and arrange and organise their courses in a way that uses television programmes as an integral part of the overall scheme.

Looking to the future we may anticipate these programmes being recorded on videotape, and thus being available to teachers as and when they are required, in the same way that films are now available.

(4) *Tape recorders*

This medium enables teachers to record planned lessons often in conjunction with worksheets geared to specific tapes. By making use of earphones and special seating plans, teachers can arrange for taped lessons to be followed by individual students or groups of

126

students while others are doing something quite different. Preparing such lessons requires considerable skill and practice on the part of the teacher. It is usually best for him to outline in detail what he wishes to cover in the lesson, to prepare an accompanying work-sheet, and to record his instructions as he works the worksheet for himself. It is important, too, not to be too intense but to include variety and humour in the tape as he would in a normal lesson. Taped lessons can be very effective as student interest is concent-rated, distracting sounds are shut out by the earphones, and neigh-bouring students are not bothered. And best of all each student is working in a one-to-one relationship with the teacher. For this reason it can be one of the most effective ways of catering for individual needs.

(5) *8 mm film loop cassettes*

These can exist by themselves or be linked to a tape so as to provide a commentary. They allow students to view a sequence as many times as necessary to understand the content. Quite an effective way sometimes is to show a loop without comment; have a discus-sion as to what has been seen; see the sequence again; further comments (?), highlights to be looked for (?); see the sequence again.

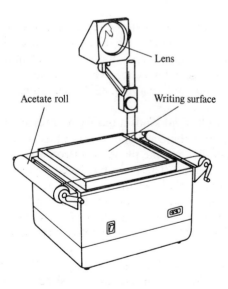

Lens

Acetate roll

Writing surface

Fig. 84. Overhead projector.

(6) *Overhead projector* (*Fig. 84*)

This instrument is one of the most flexible and potentially useful of all for work with large groups or complete classes. The material to be displayed is either written on clear acetate by the teacher in the presence of the class or can consist of a series of 'projectuals' which are laid flat on the viewing stage. A number of these can be used in succession to give overlays of different colours or shapes. This facility is enormously powerful, and represents one of the biggest advances technologically for mathematics teaching. First of all by using overlays of different colours one is able to portray a very vivid presentation of the intersection of two or more sets in a wide variety of contexts. One or two illustrations may make this clear.

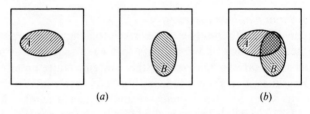

(a)   (b)

Fig. 85.

In developing Venn diagrams for sets a first projectual can consist simply of a set A; a second simply of set B (Fig. 85a). When the two are overlapped the union and intersection are immediately and clearly visible – the intersection where the colours overlap, the union the total coloured area (Fig. 85b). The extension to a third set is obvious.

For graph work of all kinds a basic grid projectual is available. Suppose in addition there are a number of other overlays consisting of a single line dividing the plane into two parts, one of which is coloured, the other not. These can be placed in position as required to show the various truth sets that conform to certain conditions. Together they illustrate the truth set for a combination of conditions, and so give an effective method of presentation for work in linear programming (Fig. 86). The uncoloured region represents the required truth set.

If one is wishing to develop a feeling for the basic quadratic form $y = ax^2 + bx + c$, an overlay consisting of the graph of the basic parabola $y = x^2$ can be made and positioned successively to

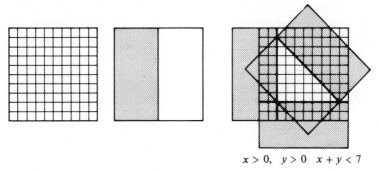

$$x > 0, \quad y > 0 \quad x + y < 7$$

Fig. 86.

illustrate what happens when we consider $y = x^2 + k$, $y = (x - a)^2$, $y = (x - a)^2 + k$, $y = -x^2$ etc. (Fig. 87). In addition a further projectual can show the parabola in terms of focus and directrix. Likewise for the other conic sections.

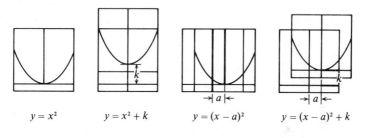

| $y = x^2$ | $y = x^2 + k$ | $y = (x - a)^2$ | $y = (x - a)^2 + k$ |

Fig. 87.

The Sieve of Eratosthenes can be shown very effectively by producing a first projectual consisting of a 'hundred square' and others consisting of coloured pattern grids to correspond to the multiples of 2, 3, 5, 7, etc. When these are laid successively over the original number square it is possible to pick out the next prime, and eventually all primes less than one hundred (Fig. 88). Work along these lines also enables us to see the set of *common multiples* of two and three, say, or of any other two numbers, and thus to speak of the *lowest common multiple* which of course is the lowest member of each such set.

Prepared projectuals can also be used to put up *tables* of information for all to see; to teach how to read slide rule scales; how to fit a

129

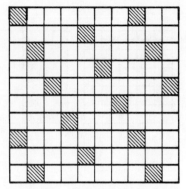

Original square with patterns
of 2, 3, and 5 superimposed

Pattern for multiples of 7

Fig. 88.

normal curve with the same mean and standard deviation as a given frequency distribution; to reproduce in the front of the class, work on rotations, reflections, etc. that the class are themselves doing by using *tracing paper*; to reproduce flow charts and computer programmes and for many other specific purposes in a wide variety of lessons.

One enormous advantage of the overhead projector is that the teacher faces and talks directly to the class and so always maintains eye contact with them. Usually no special blackout facilities are required and the teacher who operates the projector is in complete control. He can if he wishes project directly onto a *blackboard*, and then reproduce or stress with chalk aspects that appear displayed. If the projector is switched off, only these outlines remain in view.

Another use of the projector involves the presentation of material by silhouettes. An opaque shape is fastened to an acetate overlay and this, instead of being laid flat, is held at an angle to the usual plane thus giving rise to various projections of the original shape.

So there are many possibilities. However, it too frequently happens that these possibilities are not exploited, and the use of the overhead projector degenerates into nothing more imaginative than an alternative to the blackboard!

(7) *Opaque projector*

This allows projection of the coloured image of a non-transparent object. In particular one is able to project pictures or other material

130

from newspapers, periodicals or books. You may decide to use these directly with a class. Alternatively, and probably much more frequently, material from a source is projected on a surface to which one fastens some cartridge paper. The outline now visible can be traced by a felt-tip pen and so one is able to prepare accurate enlargements of visual aids, charts, diagrams, etc. to be used in subsequent lessons.

(8) *Charts, maps, graphs*
These are often obtainable directly from commercial firms and governmental agencies or can be reproduced from books and magazines by using the opaque projector. They are useful as illustration when introducing a lesson, or as material for a project or investigation, or they can be incorporated in a large scale display.

(9) *Display boards*
These should have a prominent place in any classroom and can serve a variety of purposes. Their chief advantage is that material can be left up for several days, perhaps even weeks, and can be examined by students at their leisure. But as displays form the backdrop, as it were, to the classroom, anything appearing on the boards should be attractive and well produced. They should incorporate the use of colour, novel pictures, background material, photographs, charts, maps, etc. Titles should be clear, simple, appropriate and the arrangement well thought out using devices of symmetry or deliberate imbalance, contrasts, and variations in shape and colour.

Displays often form the culmination of a group project and the preparation of such a display provides a means of stimulating creativity and craftsmanship. The planning, organisation and completing of a display involves students in working together, sharing ideas, and accepting joint responsibility. But material on notice boards can also be used as summaries of work done by the whole class, or as a means of awakening interest before a topic is introduced! Puzzles, problems, fallacies, examples of good work by students all have a place. It is important that displays should have relevance to work being done and that they should be changed frequently, otherwise their effectiveness is quickly lost.

It is often convenient to include in the display board a section of pegboard on which, by using special attachments, one can display books, or make temporary shelves for models, etc.

131

(10) *Blackboards*

By far the most commonly used of visual aids other than the text-book is the blackboard. Perhaps nowadays, chalkboard is a more appropriate title because many surfaces now have colours other than black, and the conventional slate is often replaced by some other material such as procelain steel which has the advantage that magnets adhere to it. By putting magnets on the back of pictures, models, and other materials, these can be displayed with no other adhesive required. To this extent the new surface resembles another favourite visual aid, the flannel board, which consists of a board covered usually in swansdown to which flannel, wool and other materials adhere when pressed against it. In particular newspaper cuttings and drawings made on sugar paper can be made to adhere by roughing the reverse side with emery or sand paper.

For the teaching of mathematics there should be in each class-room use a board marked out as a grid for graph work. A convenient size spacing between lines is 2 inches (or 5 centimetres). An easy way of preparing such a board is to use a sheet of hardboard, painted with an undercoat and top surface of blackboard paint and then ruled by running a sharp edge (e.g. a corner of a chisel) along a straight edge thus *scoring* the board. When chalk dust gets into these scratches they become quite clearly visible. Alternatively one can acquire a stencil on a plastic cloth which rolls up like a window shade. When this stencil is placed over an ordinary blackboard and dusted with a chalky eraser or cloth, the chalk dust passes through the stencil leaving a usable grid.

Although most teachers are aware of the basic techniques of using a board for summary, discussion, for student participation, etc. and are also aware of the need for a clear neat presentation, very often they could improve their presentation enormously by the regular use of coloured chalk. Coloured chalk can be used most effectively to identify key ideas, to add attractiveness, to emphasise common elements or to bring out contrasts and relationships. For example in work on mappings, use one colour for the object set, another for the image set; in any problem in which deductions are to be made from a drawing, use one colour to indicate facts which are known or given, another for those which can be deduced.

Another simple device which would improve the blackboard work of many teachers is the template. Outlines can be put up quickly and accurately. Alternatively before the lesson transfer to the board by means of an opaque projector a complicated outline using an ordinary lead pencil. This will be visible to you, but not to the class. When you require it, go over the pencil marks with chalk quickly and precisely.

The aids so far discussed concern either equipment which is, as it were, built into the classroom such as notice boards and blackboards, or which are relatively expensive and are often provided on the basis of one or two for the whole school, such as tape recorders, projectors of various sorts, or a combination of the two such as television receiving sets in rooms that can be partially or completely blacked out.

However another complete range of visual aids of lesser expense are *models* of various sorts. I include within this description educational apparatus which has been found to be extremely valuable in the Primary School and which could be used with profit certainly in the lower forms of the secondary school, and possibly even further up. So some structured apparatus such as Cuisenaire rods, or Colour Factor can serve as a useful aid in much of the work concerned with algebraic structure. Thus the situation represented by the rods in Fig. 89 can be interpreted in four distinct ways:

$$a + b = c \qquad c - b = a$$
$$b + a = c \qquad c - a = b$$

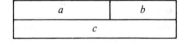

Fig. 89.

In other words whenever we can write an addition fact, we can also write a corresponding fact involving subtraction. It is only a matter of interpretation.

When we turn to the problem of recording numbers in different bases, then Dienes' Multi-base equipment (Fig. 90a) consisting of unit cubes, 'longs', 'flats', and 'blocks' is invaluable though a very adequate substitute can be made by mounting graph paper on a stiff cardboard backing, and using unit squares, long rectangles of unit width, and large squares. Instead of a cube (should its equivalent be desirable) one uses a 'super long' which bears the same relationship to the large square as the ordinary 'long' does to the unit

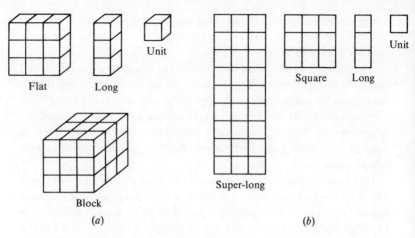

Fig. 90. *(a) Dienes' apparatus – base three; (b) a simple substitute.*

square (Fig. 90*b*). The Dienes' apparatus itself can also be used to interpret general polynomials up to the third degree where a block represents x^3, a flat x^2, a long x, and distinctions between say $2x$ and x^2 can easily be visualised.

Likewise Dienes' Logic Blocks or Attribute Blocks seem a natural, almost essential piece of equipment for early work on sets. A complete set contains pieces of four shapes, in fact prisms with circular, rectangular, square, and triangular cross-section, coloured red, blue or yellow, in two thicknesses, and in two sizes, 48 elements in all. Situations involving the intersection of up to four sets can therefore easily be created and studied. Again a simple substitute can be made of card and sticking on different shapes of different size and colour. The only attribute missing in such a set is then 'thickness', but as one is usually content to limit intersection to three sets in a Venn diagram, the apparatus is quite acceptable.

Geo-strips can serve a very useful purpose in considering the rigidity of polygons, or the building of linkages such as the pantograph. These are coloured plastic strips in various colours with holes punched in various positions, and they are joined together by using paper clips. Of course, *Meccano* serves equally as well, perhaps better because it enables three-dimensional models of very considerable complexity to be made, and special sets demonstrate gears, pulleys, levers and so on.

There has often been a feeling that such 'elementary apparatus' is out of place in a secondary school, but in fact many capable

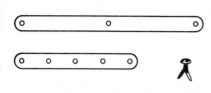

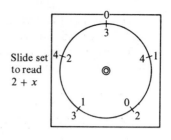

Slide set
to read
$2 + x$

Fig. 91. Geo-strips.   Fig. 92.

teachers have found that the continued use of such apparatus stimulates thinking, encourages student participation and links mathematics in a real way to the world outside. Again in the terms of Piaget, many students are still at the concrete operational stage and need to *handle apparatus* in order to think clearly.

This being so, one of the most effective methods of teaching, where it is possible, is to provide models or visual aids for everyone! So important an idea, and so simple a technique is this that I give several different illustrations.

(1) For finite arithmetics, produce circular slide rules. A circular disc of cardboard is mounted on a square of card by punching a hole through its centre, and through the back card, and then held in position with a paper fastener. Scales to the appropriate modulus are then drawn on both disc and mounting card. The centre card can now be rotated relative to the back. To *add* put the zero (0) of the centre disc opposite the first number on the back; locate the second number on the centre disc and read outwards. Fig. 92 shows the scales set to add any number to 2, modulo 5.

(2) As a strategy for teaching the addition of signed numbers, get each student to make two scales as shown in Fig. 93.

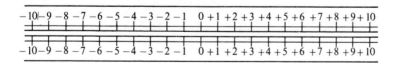

Fig. 93.

Strips cut from graph paper with squares of side 1 cm are very suitable; alternatively the *margins* from two sheets of an exercise book serve admirably.

135

To *add*, put the zero of the top scale opposite the first number, find the second number on the top scale and read down.

To *subtract*, put the *second* number on top of the *first*; find the zero of the top scale and read down.

Fig. 94.

The scales in Fig. 94 are set to show the addition of any number to -3. They can also be regarded as showing $(-9) - (-6) = -3$ etc.

(3) In studying the properties of right pyramids, either square or rectangular, let all the class make the net in Fig. 95; or produce a 'banda' stencil so that each pupil has a copy. By folding along the edges AB, BC, etc. the points V_1, V_2, V_3, V_4 are made to coincide in a single vertex V. By using a pencil to represent the altitude OV, any *triangles* needed in any calculations can easily be produced and

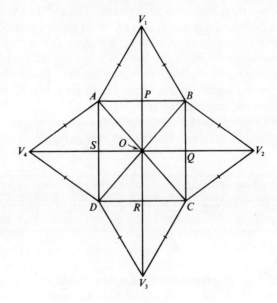

Fig. 95.

visualised, and in particular the angles which are always right angles will be clear.

(4) In studying latitude and longitude, get everyone to produce a card like that in Fig. 96.

$$\angle AOD = \angle POE = \alpha, \text{ say}$$
$$\angle BOD = \angle QOE = \beta, \text{ say}$$

Fold along the line NS, so that P falls on A, Q on B. As you gradually unfold, it is clear that the locus of P is a circle centre C_1 and radius r_1 while the locus of Q is a circle centre C_2 and radius r_2 and that $r_1 = R \cos \alpha$, and $r_2 = R \cos \beta$.

The angles of *longitude* are represented at any stage by $\angle AC_1P$ or $\angle BC_2Q$ or $\angle DOE$. For the purposes of any problem either ABD or PQE can be taken as the Greenwich meridian, depending on whether longitudes are given as east or west.

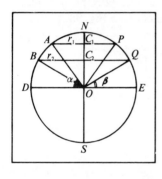

Fig. 96.

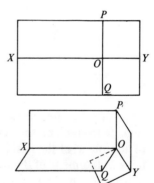

Fig. 97.

(5) For plans and elevations (first angle method) take a sheet of plain paper and fold it in half lengthwise, along XY (Fig. 97). Unfold and fold at right angles so that OQ is approximately equal to OY. Cut along OQ and fold the 'square' section under the rectangular section.

This gives every child a set of mutually perpendicular planes in which he can set various solids such as cuboids, prisms, pyramids so that he may view them from the top for the plan, and from the front and side for the elevations.

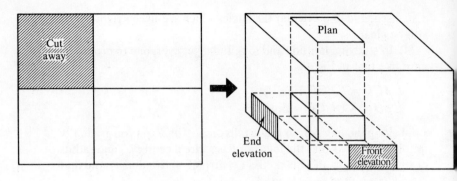

Fig. 98.

If the third angle method is being taught, the paper used should be a fairly stiff tracing paper. In this case each of the folds is exactly reversed, and one corner square completely removed. The tracing paper can then be folded to form three mutually perpendicular planes which can be placed over the object (see Fig. 98).

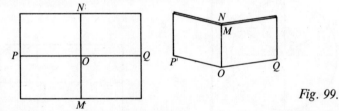

Fig. 99.

(6) Perhaps the simplest of all 'visual aids for everyman' is a piece of paper folded twice to form a right angle (Fig. 99). If this is made to stand on the desk, the common edge ON (OM) is *normal* to the plane of the desk, since it is at right angles to two distinct lines in the plane of the desk, namely OP and OQ. Moreover if the paper is opened out again so that the single fold PQ remains, the angle NOM is the angle between the *planes PNQ* and *PMQ* since both NO and OM are at right angles to the line of intersection of the two planes (Fig. 100). If the whole sheet of paper is moved so as to make the planes PNQ and PMQ coincide with any two planes say on a geometrical model, the angle between the two planes concerned can easily be seen.

(7) For much of transformation geometry, a sheet of tracing paper with an asymmetrical shape on it, preferably made up of straight lines, is invaluable.

To consider reflections about a given line, first draw the line on

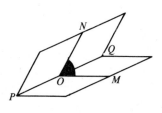

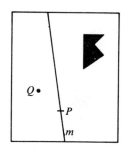

Fig. 100.   Fig. 101.

the tracing paper. Transfer both the line and the shape to the exercise book by pricking through with a pin at the vertices, and joining these points with straight lines. Be careful to mark a fixed point P on the line m (Fig. 101). Turn the tracing paper over and make line m with point P again coincide with its original position and again transfer the image with pin pricks. In the same sort of way, rotations about any point, say Q can easily be demonstrated. A 'master copy' of this process can be carried out by the teacher on the overhead projector using a sheet of clear acetate as his 'piece of tracing paper'.

Although the discussion above has implied there being a full class approach, it is clear that it can be modified for individual or group work cards, or for lessons recorded on tape, so the method is a very valuable one.

The models we have considered so far have either been produced commercially, or made as a result of the direct instructions of the teacher who uses them as a focus to his teaching. Many models, however, attain their full value as being a means of creativity, of workmanship, and skill on behalf of individual students or groups of students. Models, in this sense, also include graphs, charts, and other work produced for display by students.

One group of models in this connection arise from curve stitching. A correspondence is set up between two sets of points and the corresponding points are joined by thread. In the simplest case the points lie on two arms of an angle, and the corresponding points are labelled from opposite ends of the arms (Fig. 102). Once the technique has been understood there is plenty of opportunity for creative work in the placing of the lines, the choice of colours of thread, and even in the use of lines in three dimensions instead of

139

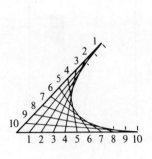

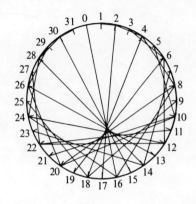

Fig. 102.   Fig. 103.

two. One can move on to consider correspondence between points on a circle. In Fig. 103 points are numbered clockwise round the circle (modulus 32) and points then chosen to correspond by the relation, 'Join point n to the point $(2n, \bmod 32)$'.

Developments along these lines lead to the development of curves by other means. For example take a point F, a line XY along which equal intervals are marked, and a set-square. Put a pin in at F and position the set-square so that side AB rests against F, and the right angle B falls on one of the marked points on XY (Fig 104). Then draw the line BC. Do this for each of the marked points. The result is an *envelope*, the parabola. Interesting modifications occur if a circle is chosen to replace the line XY. These and many other examples can be found in *A Book of Curves* by E. H.

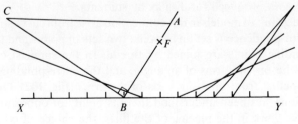

Fig. 104.

140

Fig. 105.

Lockwood (C.U.P.). Again there is no need to restrict oneself to the plane, and a most interesting model is obtained by joining corresponding points on two discs whose planes are parallel, and separated by a rod between their centres. The thread in this case should be elastic to enable one later to rotate one disc relative to the other giving rise to a hyperboloid (Fig. 105).

Another set of models that most students will want to construct at some stage of their careers is the set of five regular solids: tetrahedron, cube, octahedron, dodecahedron, and icosahedron, as well as various prisms and pyramids. The ambitious will want to go on to semi-regular solids, stellated variants and others. A full study of such models is given in *Mathematical models* by H. M. Cundy and A. P. Rollett (O.U.P.).

An interesting way of approaching many constructions is to show students a model commercially produced, or already made by someone else and ask them to prepare their own *net* together with any calculations that may be necessary. This involves them in *thinking* about the solid, its measurements and interconnections so that the work is not purely mechanical.

A useful variation in this work is to take a simple net, like that of the cube and ask how many *different* nets can be produced. In arriving at a decision as to what constitutes 'difference', ideas of rotation and reflection are involved; and if further one asks how can one record these nets without actually drawing them out in full, ideas of classification and the use of symbols are almost certain to occur.

A further category of aids which are increasingly finding a place within the classroom situation are *games* of various kinds. An adaptation of the game of *dominoes* has been mentioned in connection

141

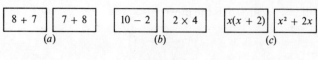

Fig. 106.

with the development of mechanical skills (p. 116). *Snap* also can be modified with cards prepared to illustrate number relations, or money value, or the distributive law or any other required skill. Some examples are given in Fig. 106. The first person to say, 'Snap' when the pairs of cards are turned over, wins them and puts them at the bottom of his pile. A third common variety which has countless variations is that where the object of the game is to collect a *set* according to some criteria or other. Conventional games of this kind are rummy, happy families, pit. These particular games have little or no mathematical significance, but clearly cards could be designed where sets could be collected according to colour or shape, or by some algebraic criteria, circles, parabolas, hyperbolas, parallel and perpendicular lines, lines passing through a given point and so on.

An ingenious mathematical game is 'Bridget'. Cards are in four suits, say circles, triangles, squares, and pentagons, and each card bears an algebraic expression (Fig. 107). Cards are dealt out as in bridge or whist and a value for x is declared either by throwing a die, spinning a wheel, drawing a card from a supplementary pile, or simply declared by the dealer. Players must follow suit where possible and as they put their cards down in order they should state their *value*. The player whose value is highest with the given x is the winner of that trick. The winner of the trick plays the first card for the next round.

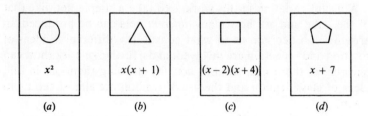

Fig. 107.

With $x = 3$, card (b) is the most valuable.

With $x = 1$, card (d) is the most valuable.

With $x = 8$, cards (b) and (c) are equal in value. In this case the *first* card played would win.

Varying degrees of complexity can be introduced with trumps, and 'bidding' and so on.

Besides such home-made games there are a large variety of commercially produced games which can play a useful part in mathematical education, e.g. *Think-a-dot, Soma Cubes*, the *Wuff' n' proof* series, various geometrical puzzles based on pentaminoes or other shapes; games using mirrors to develop insight into line symmetry, and so on. Many teachers may prefer to introduce these games first within the context of the *Mathematics Club* but may then find that some of the games can usefully be introduced within the normal classroom situation as enrichment material, or for consolidation purposes, or for reasons of motivation. [A useful book in this connection is *The maths club*, by Audrey Todd. London, Hamish Hamilton.]

Our discussion so far has largely omitted an area of considerable importance, namely that concerned with the 'practical' side of mathematics. So we need equipment for *measuring* – as applied to length, area, volume, weight, apparatus to measure force and direction, to measure time, and acceleration, the kind of apparatus more commonly found in the physics laboratory but which also has its place in the context of applications of mathematics.

Another set of materials that will often be found useful is that concerned with applications of trigonometry, and in particular surveying. So we will need compasses, angle measuring equipment varying

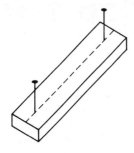

Fig. 108.

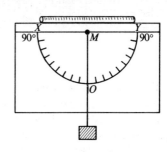

Fig. 109.

from the protractor at its simplest, through the (in)clinometer to the plane table with its alidade to possibly in some fortunate schools a theodolite. If necessary, much of this apparatus can be quite easily improvised. For a 'plane table' any flat surface will do, even an ordinary flat-topped desk. This can be levelled using an ordinary spirit level if the degree of accuracy warrants it. For an 'alidade' (Fig. 108), a simple strip of wood with two nails set along its centre line is very suitable. The distance between the nails should be 10 inches or more.

An (in)clinometer can be made from an enlarged protractor with the angles relabelled. A length of cardboard or copper tubing should be fastened along the top with its axis parallel to the *XY* line (see Fig. 109), and a weight hung from the central point *M*, using string and a drawing pin. One will also need chains, long tape measures, and sighting rods, so that applications of triangle measure in both horizontal and vertical planes can be fully appreciated.

The next range of equipment that is necessary is a variety of aids to computation. These will obviously include mathematical tables of varying degress of precision, and possibly also slide rules. In the absence of commercially produced slide rules, very adequate substitutes can be made in one of two ways. The first, which is simpler and for that reason to be preferred, is to use double cycle logarithmic paper, mounting this on card and cutting it into strips. As an *introduction* it is useful to have the two scales of different length, the bottom scale running from 1 – 100, the top from 1 – 10 only (see Fig. 110).

Fig. 110.

With these scales the rules of procedure for multiplication and division can quickly be explained and demonstrated especially if pupils have previously used 'slide rules' for addition and subtraction (p. 135), for what we are now doing essentially is to add logarithms mechanically. When this procedure has been thoroughly understood, attention may be drawn to the fact that the second cycle

144

(from 10 – 100) is an exact replica of the first cycle (from 1 – 10) and that with a slight modification of procedure we only need a single cycle for the lower scale, which for reasons of economy and convenience is the way in which slide rules are produced commercially.

If logarithmic paper is not available then the appropriate lengths can be obtained directly from a table of logarithms (multiplied by a factor of 10 to make the length of the slide rule 10 inches) as follows:

Number	Logarithm	Length from starting point to nearest hundredth of an inch
1	0.0000	0.00 inches
2	0.3010	3.01 inches
3	0.4771	4.77 inches
4	0.6021	6.02 inches
5	0.6990	6.99 inches
6	0.7782	7.78 inches
7	0.8451	8.45 inches
8	0.9031	9.03 inches
9	0.9542	9.54 inches
10	1.0000	10.00 inches
.		
.		
.		
100	2.0000	20.00 inches

Intermediate values can be found in the same way, e.g. for 3.7 the logarithm is 0.5682, and the required length from the starting point is 5.68 inches. Pupils making their own slide rules are often concerned with their own standards of accuracy, and three figure accuracy in computation with these slide rules is usually obtainable.

For some classes, particularly where children are having difficulty with multiplication, sets of Napier's rods (or bones) will be useful. These consist of a set of rods with the basic 'tables' on them, the tens and units digits being separated by a diagonal line (see Fig. 111). To multiply say 438 by 6 choose the rods 4, 3, and 8 in that order and refer to the sixth line. Starting on the right hand side, add the figures between the diagonals 'carrying' where necessary. The figures in Fig. 112 show the calculation and the result, $438 \times 6 = 2628$. In the same way by referring to the second and seventh lines we get the results of multiplying 438 by 2 and 7 respectively (Fig. 113). The method can

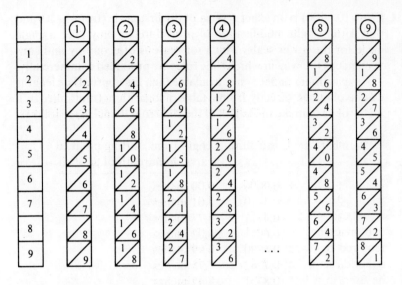

Fig. 111.

be quickly extended to long multiplication of any degree of complexity by combining lines or by writing in the *products* of each pair of numbers in the appropriate place in the required table, and adding along diagonals as before. Fig. 114 illustrates that 438 × 627 = 274626. Of course an outline of this kind should be accompanied by an explanation and discussion of *why* it works, of our use of the distributive law and of place value.

Increasingly hand calculators are finding a place amongst the commonly available equipment of schools. In the initial stages these serve a useful purpose in demonstrating the 'laws of arithmetic' such as the commutative and associative laws using *big numbers* as easily as small ones. They also clearly show the distributive property and our use of place value in the way we have to use the 'carriage shift'.

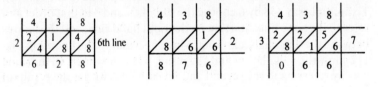

Fig. 112.   *Fig. 113.*

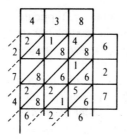

Fig. 114.

Later on they enable us to do *real* problems (i.e. using measurements from actual situations) without unnecessarily heavy mechanical arithmetic which can be tedious and time-consuming. If only one or two machines are available, almost inevitably students will be required to learn how to use them by 'individualised instruction' either direct from books or from a series of work cards. If they are to be used in a full class situation then provision at the rate of one machine between two students seems necessary.

One very important and interesting development from the use of hand calculators is the application of flow charts and an introduction to computing. A very good section showing a variety of lessons at different levels using hand calculators is to be found in *Some lessons in mathematics*, chapter 4. This also gives a useful bibliography for development of work along these lines.

With the use of such a wide variety of materials as has been outlined in this chapter, we are compelled to consider *where* it is all to be kept, and how it is best to be used, and so we come to consider establishing a mathematics specialist room, or a mathematics laboratory.

The Mathematics Laboratory

The purposes to be served by a mathematics laboratory are the following:

(*a*) It will provide a focal point within the school for mathematical knowledge and inspiration.

(*b*) It will provide facilities for incorporating experiment and practice in the learning of mathematics, and in the study of its related applications.

(*c*) It will provide a centre of mathematical information. It can do this partly through the inclusion of a mathematical library, which

147

might replace, supplement, or duplicate the collection of mathematics books in the main school library, and partly through the inclusion of collections of models, diagrams and visual representations of mathematical concepts.

Ideally a special room should be designed to enable all these things to take place. The plan and specification given in the appendix is reproduced from a pamphlet *Mathematical laboratories in schools* prepared for the Mathematical Association. It will be noted that the following particular facilities have been kept in mind:

(i) Adequate storage with access *by students* to commonly required materials such as graph paper, scissors, paste, drawing boards.

(ii) Easily movable furniture with flat top surfaces that can be combined or pulled apart as required to enable varieties of groupings of students for different projects to take place. In particular both 'formal' and 'informal' full class and small groupings are possible.

(iii) Sufficient electrical and blackout facilities to enable all the more specialised apparatus described earlier in the chapter to be used effectively.

(iv) Plenty of display space and a variety of surfaces on which to put these displays.

(v) Provision for model making, to enable children to cut, drill, glue, paint, solder, and assemble.

(vi) Availability of water and a sink both for experiments requiring water for their own sake, and for adequate tidying up after other activities.

These considerations show that even when no specialist room is provided much can be done with an ordinary classroom to convert it to this specialist role. The starting point is the *furniture*, flat-topped tables easily movable and capable of being set out in a variety of ways together with stackable chairs that give more room for movement when the chairs are not actually being used. Next comes display facilities, blackout, electrical points, and storage. All storage facilities should be labelled clearly and pupils encouraged to return apparatus to its 'right place' after use.

When and if such a room has been specially provided or adapted from an ordinary classroom, then it would appear essential that every class should have 'workshop sessions' (i.e. double periods or longer) in this room, so that the best possible use is made of the specialist facilities and so that every student gets the encouragement of seeing mathematics in the making. This room will also automatically become the focus for any Mathematics Club the school may have, and the Club may well be a source of further apparatus, material and games for use in normal curriculum work.

The Mathematics Library
Closely allied to the mathematics laboratory is the mathematics library. Some will feel that a suitable section in the main library is all that is required; others will feel that suitable provision made *geographically close* to the laboratory is very much more advantageous, as it can then be related more directly to work done in the laboratory, or to projects assigned during class work.

In either case one goes to the library because in it one hopes to find books which are intrinsically interesting in themselves, or because it contains books which will assist one in one's work or hobbies, or in order to further one's own studies. This is true not only of the student at school but of every educated person who has left school; and it would appear to be one of the aims of education to instil in students an attitude towards books and libraries that will ensure their continued use throughout life. It is valuable therefore that members of staff should be seen to be using the library themselves as well as encouraging students to do so.

So it is important that the library should contain books which are useful to the teacher, books on methodology, background, mathematical education, history, books of puzzles and amusements, some of the material from which can be incorporated into his teaching. Then there should be books for the use of more advanced students so that something of the reaching forward to horizons far beyond that of any current syllabus can be realised by those who wish. But of course the bulk of the library will be books for general use and of general interest.

They will include books on the history of mathematics and mathematical ideas, books presenting mathematics from an unusual or popular standpoint, books linking mathematics with other subjects, with astronomy, philosophy, geography, science, industry, business management, with hobbies of various kinds. There will be reference books, nautical tables, Whitaker's Almanack, other statistical tables, and a selection of books with original contributions by famous mathematicians either in their entirety or incorporating a judicious choice. There will be books written very much for the classroom and for use by students in developing and enriching their own mathematical education.

The teacher in charge can get much help in keeping his stock up to date by reference to such publications as a *School Library Mathematics List* sponsored by the Mathematics Association and published by G. Bell & Sons, by reading reviews in various professional journals, and by recommendations from colleagues.

Summary
In this chapter we have considered various sources and kinds of material which will give substance and variety to the presentations we devise under strategy and method. They vary from the relatively expensive – projectors and survey equipment, to the very cheap – paper, pencil and glue; and from the generally available such as textbooks and chalkboard to the relatively rare such as desk calculators. To utilise resources effectively, whatever they are, we have seen the value of having a central mathematics laboratory and library. Moreover where these are available we have seen how important it is that all students have at least *some* of their classes in this specialist area.

8. Evaluation

In the opening chapter which outlined the teaching process, evaluation was seen as the final stage in any given section of 'teaching'. The point was made that evaluation always has two aspects, the first relating to one's performance as a teacher and the second to the level of attainment achieved by individual pupils. Both aspects can only be satisfactorily evaluated if the teacher has a clear idea of objectives for without clear objectives it is impossible to say whether a satisfactory standard has been reached or not.

In later chapters outlining content, strategy and method the point was made that preparation for teaching occurs at four distinct levels: (1) plans for a complete course; (2) the scheme of work for a year or term; (3) the unit lesson plan and (4) the daily lesson plan. Quite clearly therefore, evaluation must also take place at all these levels, and in fact in a sense at a fifth level – the level of actual communication with children. For even as we are speaking, explaining, we must have at the back of our minds questions like these: 'Is this going across? Am I being understood? Would other vocabulary, structure, modes of speech be more appropriate? Is there a question I could ask to help children approach things from a different tack, or help them to reach the next stage in an argument or development?' The answer to these questions more often than not is found in the expressions on pupils' faces: a relaxed, interested, committed, engrossed attitude when something is being well taught; an air of puzzlement, disbelief, or complete indifference when things are not going as they should. It is reflected also in their actions – a concentration on the activity concerned when they are fully involved; frivolity, unnecessary noise, restlessness and fidgeting when they are not. Evaluation, therefore is always with us, but at certain times it must be more specific than at others.

Let us, as it were, reverse the order of preparation and consider evaluation on an ascending scale, working from the daily lesson, to the unit, to the year's work, and to a complete course.

At the conclusion of any lesson or period of activity, in reflecting upon it, the teacher must ask himself a number of questions, the first of which is, 'Did I do what I set out to do?' If the answer is 'No',

151

these are some of the follow-up questions he might ask himself: Was it because the strategy was wrong? Would a different approach be worth trying? Was it because the *organisation* of the class was inadequate? Or because instructions were not clear? Were the pupils not sure what to do? Were the work cards ambiguous? Was I trying to take too big a step? Had I allowed enough time and practice for consolidation of previous work? Was my timing at fault? Did I talk too much, and not give the pupils enough time doing mathematics? Would it be worth seeking advice from a colleague?

If the answer to the original question was 'Yes', these are some of the questions one might go on to consider: Was success because of the method? Or because of some particular question (or series of questions)? Or because of some contribution from a student (or students)? Is there anything worth recording for future reference? Would anyone else be interested in hearing of the development of this particular lesson?

A second question that must be asked at the conclusion of every lesson is, 'What points from this lesson must be borne in mind in preparing for the next lesson with this class?' This question may be broken down into others: Will any revision be necessary? Will it be useful to incorporate a test of some kind? Is there some point that I might have made today but didn't that ought to be included next time? Can the *same* class organisation continue, or do I need a different one – a rearrangement of groupings, or further work cards?

Most of the questions that have been posed so far have been purely subjective and refer to 'success in achieving one's objective'. This success may be apparent in general class atmosphere, in the reluctance of children to stop doing what they are engaged in, in spontaneous after-lesson questions; but there must, of course, periodically also be an objective assessment, some way of measuring what learning has taken place on the part of the various children in the class.

This aspect of the amount and kind of learning that has taken place becomes increasingly important as we move up the scale from daily lessons to the unit or topic, from that to the work of a term or of a year, and ultimately to a complete school course. We must consider, therefore, the place, purpose and assessment of different kinds of work done by pupils and then move on to the whole question of records and of examinations.

The work that children do, and the written record they produce of that work, is assigned for a variety of different reasons, and it is important that assessment should relate to *those* reasons, and not to some other externally imposed criteria such as producing an 'order of merit' list. The difficulty of trying to produce such a list is that within the realm of any subject and particularly in the case of mathematics, there are so many different facets to both the process of learning and the content of the course that a single concluding mark or grade cannot possibly give a picture of the ability or progress of any individual. What we shall be working towards, therefore, is a *profile* of a child under various headings so as to draw attention to strengths and weaknesses, and to help the child himself to come to self-awareness of his own virtues and failings.

One such form of profile is that in use at Brentwood Secondary School where the headings under which assessments are made in each subject are as follows: Knowledge, Understanding, Skills, Originality, Neatness, Oral, Co-operation, Perseverance, Self-understanding. The rubric which accompanies the pro-forma is reproduced below.

'These assessments are based on the teachers' observations over a period of the pupil's work, attitude and ability in class. They give a more complete profile than is obtained from the usual assessment based on performance in terminal examinations, though they may be supplemented by various tests. It is intended that they should be used to find and develop a pupil's strengths rather than to emphasise weaknesses. The five-point scale is applied to the whole of a year group in which there will be approximately 5% in the A (excellent), 20% in the B (good), 50% in the C (average), 20% in the D (below average) and 5% in the E category. The abilities assessed are as follows:

1. *Knowledge*
The ability to memorise the facts connected with the subject, topic or activity.
2. *Understanding*
Ability to apply the facts learnt. Powers of deduction. Ability to recognise problems and choose appropriate means to solve them.
3. *Skills*
Acquisition of skills applicable to the particular activity or subject, e.g. ability to write grammatically or spell correctly, to calculate, use tools correctly, the techniques of painting or drawing as opposed to the creative or imaginative side.
4. *Originality*
Powers of creativity and original thought. Initiative.

5. *Neatness*
How the work is presented. Layout, order, arrangement, etc.
6. *Oral*
Ability to take part in discussion and express a point of view.
7. *Co-operation*
Ability to accept others, to pool knowledge and work co-operatively in groups. (This also includes attitude to authority and readiness to obey or take command if required.)
8. *Perseverance*
Conscientiousness. Progress over a period. Persistence, etc.
9. *Self-Understanding*
Realistic self-understanding and self-acceptance. Self-disciplining when required by needs of others or an activity. Self-forgetting, curiosity and enjoyment.

It will be noted that there are a certain number of behavioural objectives which apply regardless of content within a subject and even of a subject itself, notably those concerned with social awareness and relationships with others. With such a profile in mind we can return to the different types of activity that children engage in and consider what constitutes appropriate evaluation.

By far the most common kind of work that children 'hand in' is answers to written exercises, and the majority of these exercises, are set either to consolidate understanding of a concept or to develop facility in a skill. If the purpose of the exercise is the *first* of these, then it is absolutely essential that the work be examined in detail and as quickly as possible. So if the exercise is set during class, the teacher should go round looking at the work as children do it, helping where there is difficulty. Ticks for correct work are appropriate, but crosses for incorrect work are not! What is required is *help*, not criticism, and if an answer is wrong then some sort of comment like, 'That's not quite right; let's look at it together' is what is required. Very often if it is only a mechanical slip, a ring round the place where the mistake has taken place is the most useful for it focusses a child's attention on the error and enables him to correct it for himself.

When such work is handed in to be corrected out of class, my own view is that the same procedures apply, and that children should be encouraged to find their own mistakes and put them right. In the case where there are no ticks and no circles, they should be asked to do the question again, or one like it. No child will then have the psychologically distressing situation of having an exercise book full of crosses. Instead there should be only pages of ticks!

The appropriate record in one's 'mark book' is probably a tick ($\sqrt{}$) if the work is clearly understood, a blank (. . .) if it is not, (i.e. waiting until you *can* put in a tick), and a ($\sqrt{}-$) if understanding seems to be coming but is not yet complete, and extra work such as a few corrections are required. A further symbol, perhaps ($\bigcirc$) may be useful to indicate that work has not been submitted, and a follow-up is necessary.

NAMES	Ex. 34	Ex. 35	Ex. 36
Adam	$\sqrt{}$	$\sqrt{}$	$\sqrt{}$
Benjamin	$\sqrt{}$		
Christopher	$\sqrt{}-$	$\sqrt{}$	$\sqrt{}$
David	$\bigcirc$	$\bigcirc$	
Ephraim	$\sqrt{}$	$\sqrt{}-$	
. . . .			
. . . .			
. . . .			

If the purpose of the exercise is *merely practice*, that is, when it can be assumed that there is real understanding but there is need to develop further facility, then some method of self-pacing is appropriate. For example a personal graph could be kept at the back of the exercise book of the number of questions done correctly within a given time; or the time taken to set out a complete of dominoes, or go through a set of flash cards with a friend (see p. 116). It should be noted that an exercise originally set for understanding, later can become an exercise used for practice drill after you have made sure that everyone has got them all right at least once. Certainly at this stage there is much to be said for students having access to answers.

One part of the recording process in the case of group practical work has already been discussed (p. 120) but there will be a subsequent need to look at the individual's work within a group. The main points here are to ensure as far as possible that the purpose of the card has been understood and to try to develop standards of

155

presentation and neatness. In fact one may feel that a letter grade A, B, C, or D would be appropriate in this case. Points that occur to you as being worthy of the attention of the whole group or class should be set down for incorporation in your next lesson plan. On the other hand, points that refer to individuals alone may be dealt with either by a direct written comment, or by a phrase such as 'See me' if you feel that spoken comment is more appropriate, either because it would take too long to write out all your remarks, or because you feel the need to ask questions about particular points before making further comments.

If a system of individualised work cards is used either as the main method of instruction or to supplement the work of textbooks, a suitable record must be devised so that progress and development are seen to be taking place, and to ensure that undue repetition does not occur. Here completion of cards would be recorded in one's mark book in much the same way as the exercise numbers in a more traditional situation, e.g. the headings might be as follows:

	MATRICES							
	A_1	A_2	A_3	B_1	B_2	C_1	C_2	C_3
Pupil A	✓	✓		✓		✓		
Pupil B	✓		✓	✓	✓		✓	
Pupil C	✓	✓		✓	✓	✓		
....								

Projects, and investigations normally serve a quite different purpose from the kind of work discussed so far. The headings for our assessment here are likely to be the following: Effort, understanding, originality, powers of organisation, neatness; possibly also co-operation with others.

Effort, understanding and neatness can be assessed by other activities, but originality, and powers of organisation, that is of material, into a logical, coherent, account perhaps involving argument and proof are aspects which do not arise naturally in other contexts. It is clearly important, therefore that some work along these lines be done. It is also important that fairly comprehensive and detailed comment be made about each child's work. I think this is best made on a separate sheet of paper which the child can keep, either with the piece of work or separately as he feels inclined. These comments, according to how specific they are, are the means by which a child gradually acquires the ability to criticise his own work, to recognise latent abilities like draughtsmanship and neatness, to learn to re-organise and re-present work in a more coherent way; and to appreciate the finer points of mathematical presentation and proof, the virtues of brevity, conciseness, suitable symbolism. All these are essential ingredients in a true mathematical education.

We come now to the place of tests and examinations. If there is a distinction at all between these, it is that tests are seen as an integral part of the teaching situation while an examination in some sense represents the culmination of instruction, the final act as it were, and its outcome is taken as a measure of achievement of success for the course as a whole.

This difference is important, for in fact one can imagine a number of different kinds of test all serving different purposes. Amongst these are the following:

(1) *Open book tests*
Here, since any *factual* information one may require is accessible, the emphasis is on understanding, and of application of ideas to new problems.

(2) *Reading tests*
The idea of these tests is to comprehend a situation and convert it into mathematical terms. It corresponds in a sense to a 'translation' paper in a language.

(3) *Performance tests*
These relate chiefly to practical skills, and the ability to achieve certain standards of accuracy in the use of certain equipment.

(4) *Essays*
These emphasise communication skills, and the ability to integrate and present ideas clearly.

(5) *Attitude tests*
Though often highly suspect, their purpose is to try to appraise attitudes towards a subject or occupation. Some sort of attitude testing is often used in counselling.

157

(6) *Achievement tests*

These vary from simple 'quizzes' on the work of a single period to full-scale examinations which we will discuss later. They can be sub-divided perhaps into 'free response' and 'multiple-choice' tests.

(7) *Diagnostic tests*

The chief purpose of these is to locate areas of misunderstanding or areas where teaching has not taken place to enable suitable remedial instruction to be given.

(8) *Inventory tests*

These are perhaps more commonly referred to as 'pre- and post-tests'. They are used particularly in research situations where a *measure of improvement* is required, and the same (or similar) tests are given before and after the courses of instruction, any change being attributed to the effectiveness or otherwise of the course.

(9) *Prognostic or aptitude tests*

These are designed to try to predict future performance often on the basis of an observed correlation between two or more skills.

(10) *Tests of creativity*

These tests attempt to test and analyse creativity by presenting a situation in which a starting point is given but no fixed end point is pre-determined.

(11) *Contest tests*

These differ from all the previous tests in that some sort of prize is expected by the highest achievers.

(12) *Practice tests*

The purpose of these tests is to accustom candidates psychologically to the conditions of any other kind of test they may later be subjected to!

In designing tests of any kind there are a number of criteria that ideally we would like to fulfil. We want tests if possible to be valid, reliable, fair, to discriminate well between candidates, to be comprehensive and as far as possible to be easy to administer and score. Let us examine each of these criteria a little more closely.

Validity

The idea here is that the test really does measure what it sets out to; if it is an achievement test that it measures achievement; if a prognostic test, that it does reveal potentiality; if a diagnostic test, that it does reveal weaknesses that can be put right. The requirements for each of these different tests are often quite distinct, and yet a trap that we are all inclined to fall into is to think that somehow or other *one* test can fulfil all these purposes. This is particularly so with examination results at the conclusion of a secondary school course. The examinations themselves are basically achievement tests, but the results are frequently used for other purposes such as a basis for selection procedures, either for further education or employment. Strictly speaking these are not valid uses of these examination scores unless the examination has been *designed* to fulfil these purposes.

Reliability

If a test were 100% reliable then any candidate's score would be immutable. He would score the same if he took the examination today as if he took it tomorrow. Clearly this ideal is unobtainable. The best that can be done is to reduce the variation in scores by curbing factors which spoil the perfect testing situation. The main factors which contribute to measurement error, and therefore depress reliability are these:

(*a*) Actual changes in the examinees' mental and physical states which affect their examination performances.

(*b*) Inadequate sampling of the examinee's knowledge and ability by the particular questions set.

(*c*) Inconsistencies in the standard of marking adopted by different examiners (in the case of large-scale examinations) or by the same examiner on different occasions.

(*d*) Differences of opinion (particularly in essay-type questions) as to the relative merit of examinee's answers.

Thus *any score* should not be regarded as absolute, but rather as a measurement which is accurate to within a given range, in much the same way as measures of length are never exact, but accurate to within a given margin of error.

Fairness

It is possible that a test might satisfy high standards of validity and reliability and still not be fair. Fairness is a quality which is recognised by candidates; it relates to the whole impression that they get of a paper, whether it is 'on the syllabus', whether the standard expected is too hard or ridiculously simple, whether there is a reasonable amount of time, and so on. If a paper is not *seen* to be fair, then its results are inevitably called into question.

Discrimination

One of the chief purposes of tests and examinations is to discriminate between the ability of candidates. A paper in which every candidate got the same mark would clearly serve no useful purpose. On the other hand too wide a spread can sometimes be misleading. In most school situations it is important to realise that the *range* or *spread* of marks in any paper is also of the greatest significance in any totalling of marks; the greater the spread, the greater the weighting given to the paper concerned. Thus in general terms if the spread of marks in History is 40, while that in Mathematics is 80, then effectively the marks in mathematics are weighted twice as heavily as those in history in any grand total. This is so regardless of the *average mark* in each paper provided that all candidates sit both papers.

Being comprehensive

This relates to measuring *every aspect* that is meant to be covered by the test concerned. Thus if it is an examination at the conclusion of a course it must be concerned with trying to assess progress towards *each* of the aims or objectives set out at the beginning of the course. It is unfortunately true that certain aspects of achievement are much more readily testable than others, and that often those results which are measurable are taken as indicative of prowess in other areas which may or may not be the case.

Ease of administration and scoring

This aspect becomes increasingly important as the size of the operation increases. If we are dealing with small numbers, then it may not appear to be of great significance, but in the case of large examination bodies, it is of the utmost importance. No-one likes to wait unnecessarily long for the results of any test, and if we are to mark thirty to forty thousand scripts then procedures which ease administration and scoring are much to be welcomed, provided of course that such procedures don't violate the other requirements outlined above.

Of all the many types of test the ones that we, as classroom practitioners are most concerned with, are achievement tests. We may use these periodically as checks on progress during the year; we will probably have an expanded form of such a test in termly examinations, and will certainly be expected to have one (or its equivalent) at the end of each year. If we consider preparations and procedures for this final examination we should, in passing, determine principles for those of lesser consequence also.

The first step is to state clearly, in concise operational terms, the *objectives* of instruction. This is not an unreasonable demand; people are constantly doing it in other spheres of life. Thus the optician starts with the aim of measuring the overall effectiveness of eyesight, but this aim is broken down into a number of lesser enquiries: Can the patient perceive all the colours? What is the range of his vision? How good is his discrimination? And so on. To answer these questions the optician devises a series of tasks which the patient is invited to tackle, and from the patient's responses the optician gets a differential profile of eye capacity which enables him to prescribe with great precision, the corrective treatment the patient should have.

The objectives now referred to are more precise still than those discussed in Chapters 2 and 3. Each objective should fulfil the following conditions. It should be:

(*a*) described in operational terms,
(*b*) observable,
(*c*) verifiable, and
(*d*) assessable by a pencil and paper test or some other means.

Thus a statement such as 'knows decimals' is not precise enough, but would have to be broken up into more precise components such as:

Understands the meaning of the decimal point.
Can add and subtract numbers involving decimals.
Can multiply and divide numbers involving decimals.
Can apply decimal notation to problem situations.

Most objectives can be grouped into categories under some general description such as *Knowing, Manipulating, Applying*, etc. This helps to hold terms in place and give a reference system for communication with other teachers. There are, as it were, two main dimensions in achievement testing, one of subject matter and the other of process, i.e. the behaviour a student is expected to display if he has achieved the objectives. The most practical form of analysis is a two dimensional grid set out in outline in Fig. 115.

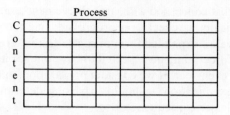

Fig. 115.

When the grid has been filled out it gives a picture of a curriculum and at the same time a blue-print for the design of an achievement test.

Various classifications have been used in describing behaviour. It is often broken down into three interacting areas, roughly corresponding to thinking, feeling, and acting. The first to make a definitive contribution in the thinking area or *cognitive domain* was Professor B. S. Bloom in his *Taxonomy of educational objectives.* The generic term, 'taxonomy' was carefully chosen by Bloom and his co-workers to indicate that their classification possessed certain characteristics. For instance, the objectives are organised in such a way that each category is built upon and depends on its predecessors.

Others building on this work have tried to simplify the classification. In an international evaluation of achievement study* the five categories of objective adopted were:

A. *Knowledge and Information*: recall of definitions, notations, concepts.
B. *Techniques and Skills:* computation, manipulation of symbols.
C. *Comprehension:* capacity to understand problems, to translate symbolic forms, to follow and extend reasoning.
D. *Application* of appropriate concepts to unfamiliar mathematical situations.
E. *Inventiveness:* reasoning creatively in mathematics.

Another classification put forward by the Schools Mathematics Study Group in the United States is the following:

---

*International Study of Achievement in Mathematics (1967), edited by Torsten. Stockholm (Almqvist and Wicksell) and New York (Wiley), Vol. I, Ch. 4.

LEVELS OF INTELLECTUAL ACTIVITY IN MATHEMATICS

KNOWING:	knowing terminology, facts and rules
TRANSLATING	changing from one language to another
	expressing ideas in verbal, symbolic, or geometric forms
	codifying patterns
MANIPULATING	carrying out algorithms
	using techniques
CHOOSING	making comparisons
	selecting appropriate facts and techniques
	guessing
	estimating
	changing one's approach
	selecting new symbolism
ANALYZING	analyzing data
	finding differences
	recognizing relevant and irrelevant information
	seeing patterns, isomorphisms, and symmetries
	analyzing proofs
	recognizing need for additional information
	recognizing need for proof or counter example
SYNTHESIZING	specializing and generalizing
	conjecturing
	formulating problems
	constructing a proof or a problem
	validating answers
	judging reasonableness of answers
EVALUATING	validating the solution process
	criticizing proofs
	judging the significance of a problem

The Committee responsible for the setting of the University of London GCE Ordinary level in Mathematics Syllabus C, in devising their multiple-choice paper, rather than describing behaviour, refer to the following categories of ability:

Ability 0   The ability to recall factual knowledge
Ability 1   The ability to perform mathematical manipulations
Ability 2   The ability to solve routine problems

Ability 3   The ability to demonstrate comprehension of mathematical ideas and concepts

Ability 4   The ability to solve non-routing problems requiring insight or ingenuity, and the ability to apply higher mental processes to mathematics.

The main point, however, is that the attempt is made to break down behaviour into smaller, measurable, units. This can, in fact, give rise to a means of balancing a syllabus. Suppose for example, we decide to talk of behaviour characteristics A, B, C, D and E, and on examining topics 1, 2, 3, 4, 5 and 6 arrive at the following analysis, where a 1 indicates that a particular topic can be used to elicit a certain behaviour:

Behaviours

		A	B	C	D	E
T	1	1		1		
O	2	1	1	1	1	1
P	3			1		
I	4	1		1	1	
C	5	1	1			1
S	6	1		1		1

It is clear that topic 3 is not contributing much to the overall development and might very well be omitted. Likewise also topic 1. In this way, by concentrating on the content needed to secure the desired behaviour, the syllabus could be thinned out, and some attention given to arranging it to achieve optimum learning efficiency.

When we come to design a test, we need to decide on the relative emphases we wish to give to various content areas and objectives. This weighting should normally be directly related to the amount of time we have spent on the areas in our teaching. Suppose for example we decide that our weighting should be as follows:

Objectives of instruction	*Percentage of items (marks)*
A. Knowledge	20
B. Skills	25

C. Comprehension   25
D. Application   20
E. Inventiveness   10

Content	Percentage of items (marks)
1. Arithmetic	30
2. Algebra	30
3. Geometry	30
4. Statistics	10

These would be combined in a two-way table as follows:

Objectives of instruction

		A	B	C	D	E	Total
	1						30
Content	2						30
	3						30
	4						10
		20	25	25	20	10	100

When designing and choosing questions we try to ensure that processes and marks are allocated so that the appropriate totals down and across are attained.

This work, of course, is considerably simplified if we use 'multiple-choice' questions, for generally speaking each question will fit uniquely into the grid testing one item of content and one process. It will, if you like, have content-process 'co-ordinates'. This is one of the reasons that multiple-choice papers are now so much more frequently used. There are others and it may be convenient to summarise these:

(*a*) A multiple-choice paper contains a much greater number of questions than a conventional paper. It therefore more readily satisfies the criterium of *being comprehensive*.

(*b*) A multiple-choice paper is constructed to an agreed specification, and a definite weighting can be given to each syllabus topic and mathematical ability. In so far as these abilities meet the original aims and objectives the paper is likely to be more *valid*.

165

(*c*) The mark gained by a candidate is simply the total number of questions he has answered correctly. This eliminates some of the difficulties outlined under *reliability*. In fact suitably designed papers can be scored and analysed completely by computer, thus in addition considerably *easing and speeding up the process of scoring*.

Other advantages can occur when there is a large team engaged in their design and administration. These are that multiple-choice questions can be pre-tested and it can be known that the questions used are *unambiguous* and that they *discriminate* well between candidates. Moreover pre-testing also shows the difficulty level of each question so that it is possible to construct a paper of the right length and difficulty for the candidate population.

Two major points emerge from the previous paragraphs: (1) the fact that *not all* objectives readily lend themselves to assessment by multiple-choice questions, or indeed by examination at all, and (2) that after testing, comes analysis. Both of these require further discussion.

Let us first follow through the test or examination beyond the point where marks have been allocated and scores obtained. There should now follow an analysis. It is usually best when working with a single class to arrange scripts in order of merit, and then in a table like that below to record the break-down of the allocation of marks by questions. This procedure incidentally also provides a check to one's totalling of marks! The illustration given assumes that all questions are compulsory, that there has been no element of choice, and that the paper was of a standard free-response problem type. A zero indicates that the question has been tried but no marks obtained for it, while a blank indicates that it has been omitted altogether.

When we look carefully at a break-down like this, we notice a number of things. First of all there are those questions reasonably well answered by the majority. With the limited evidence below this would be true of questions 1, 2, 5*a*, 9 and possibly 6. These questions indicate areas that have been well taught and are generally understood. Next there are questions, or parts of questions so difficult that virtually no-one scores on it, e.g. 7*b* and 7*c*. This kind of situation reveals work that should be re-taught. Then there are questions which seems to be well answered by the good students while the poorer ones either score poorly or don't attempt it at all, such as 4*a* and 4*b*, 5*b*, 7*a* and 10. Such questions are said to 'discriminate' well, as they are the ones which give rise to the bulk of variation in the total scores.

Analysis of an examination paper

Question	1	2	3	4 a	4 b	5 a	5 b	6	7 a	7 b	7 c	8	9	10	Total
Full marks	6	7	8	5	5	5	5	12	4	5	6	10	10	12	100
1st pupil	6	7	8	5	5	5	5	8	4	5	4	10	10	10	92
2nd pupil	6	7	8	5	4	5	5	10	4	5	0	10	10	9	88
3rd pupil	6	7	8	5	5	5	4	12	4	0	0	10	8	6	80
4th pupil	6	6	8	4	4	5	5	10	4	0	0	10	10	8	78
.															
.															
.															
28th pupil	6	4	4	2	0	2		6				3	8	0	35
29th pupil	4	7	3	0	0	5						4	8		31
30th pupil	4	7	0	0	0	3		6				0	6		26

In the case of multiple-choice questions this analysis can be very much more precise, as questions are either right or wrong. The proportion of candidates who get a question right is indicative of its ease or facility, or as it is referred to by the University of London Examination Board its p-value. Thus if 47% of candidates answer the question correctly its p-value would be 0.47. Normally where pre-testing takes place most questions have a p-value between 0.20 and 0.80 as they are otherwise too difficult or too easy.

Discrimination is measured in a number of ways. One of the simplest is to divide the class in half (in the case of odd numbers of candidates omitting the candidate with the median score). To each question a value, H is assigned corresponding to the number of candidates in the upper half of the class who answer the question correctly; likewise a value, L is given to the number of candidates in the lower half of the class who answer the question correctly, and the value d (discrimination factor) calculated by the formula:

$$d = \frac{H - L}{N}$$ where $N = n(H)$ or $n(L)$, the number in each group

Let us take a numerical example. In a class of 30, 14 in the upper half of the class get a certain question right, while only 5 in the lower half answer it correctly, i.e. $H = 14$, $L = 5$, and $N = 15$.

$$\text{Thus } d = \frac{14 - 5}{15} = 0.6.$$

Other variants of the discrimination factor take the highest and lowest thirds or quarters, but otherwise use the same procedure.

Clearly the higher the value of d, the better the discrimination. It is, of course, possible to get *negative* values for d if more candidates in the lower half of a class get a question right than in the upper. This is usually indicative of some ambiguity in the wording of the question which makes one of the 'distractors' seem correct to the more able, while the subtlety is missed by the less able. Such questions, of course, would be modified or omitted after pre-testing. Usually values of d must be greater than 0.2 before questions are accepted for future use.

When questions are pre-tested it is possible to assign a p-value and a d-value to every question, and hence to design examinations of any given degree of difficulty (by choosing questions according to their p-value) and at the same time to ensure that they discriminate reasonably well. If in addition questions are 'filed' according to their place in the Content–Process table, one can conceive of a situation where an item-bank is established, and teachers could ask for questions to cover both topic and process and to be of the required standard of difficulty! [An experiment along these lines is described by R. Wood in an article *Research into assessment – the item bank project* in the A.T.M. pamphlet *Examinations and assessment*.]

We can now summarise the procedures associated with testing in a flow chart (Fig. 116). It will be noted that after the item analysis

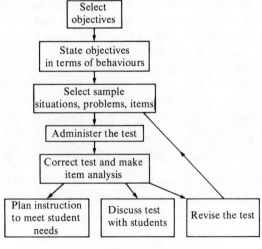

Fig. 116.

the teacher has three duties: to discuss the test with his students so that they may see their own mistakes and correct them; to plan instruction to include re-teaching of those areas which have been badly understood by the majority; and lastly to modify the structure, form and questions in any test prepared for a comparable group on another occasion.

We must now return to the problem implicit in the third step in this process. Can conventional and/or multiple-choice questions in examinations really test *all* the objectives we have? Clearly multiple-choice questions have the limitation that they cannot effectively test abilities such as the power to sustain a mathematical argument. It is for this reason that the Universities Entrance and School Examinations Council of London University has laid down that a multiple-choice paper shall form only part of any examination. But even the conventional papers which certainly can require consecutive stages of argument or proof, frequently do not test all the skills we hope to develop in students. Among these is the skill of collecting necessary and sufficient information to solve a problem. This is an ability worth testing, and might be done with a question like this:

A well of water is supplied by a spring, and water supplies for a village are pumped from this well. How deep is the water in the well when the pump has been running for three hours?
List the information you might need to solve the above problem.

It sometimes happens that necessary information cannot be obtained, and then *assumptions* have to be made. Different assumptions give rise to different answers, and questions can be written quite easily which test a pupil's ability to make reasonable assumptions and to compare their outcomes. For example,

Towns A and B are connected by road and railway. The distance by road is 300 miles, by rail 280 miles. Costs when travelling by car can be taken to be calculated on the basis of depreciation at 50p each day, petrol at 35p a gallon and oil at 20p a pint; while rail fares are 2p a mile for adults, and children are taken at half price. By making various assumptions, and listing them, calculate whether it is cheaper for four people to travel together by car or rail from A to B.

169

Another skill which is rarely tested but is valuable, is that of recognising what problems one can solve with given information and of deriving further information from that given. Below is a question testing this skill:

(a) *A certain town has a population of 120 000.*

(b) *30% of the population are children.*

(c) *At the last election there was a 70% turnout of all the adult population.*

(d) *The candidate from Party A defeated the candidate from Party B by 1200 votes.*

Derive four more pieces of information from those given.

We are on the verge here of testing creative skills, the kind of ability normally associated with investigations. Attempts have been made to incorporate these also into an examination structure where there is no great pressure of time. One such paper is given below:

MATHEMATICAL SYLLABUS (SPECIAL)

Paper II

Four hours allowed

Answer **one** *question only.*

1. Investigate, algebraically rather than geometrically, the set of matrices

$$\left\{ \begin{pmatrix} a & b \\ c & d \end{pmatrix}; a + b = c + d \right\};$$

e.g. $\begin{pmatrix} 3 & 2 \\ 1 & 4 \end{pmatrix}$ belongs to the set, since $3 + 2 = 4 + 1$ and so does

$\begin{pmatrix} 3 & 8 \\ -1 & 12 \end{pmatrix}$ since $3 + 8 = -1 + 12 = 11$.

2. The first eight binary numbers, i.e. those with three 'bits', may be arranged in order so that only one bit is changed at a time, and the last one may be changed back to zero in the same way. An order which works for the eight numbers is

$$\begin{array}{c}
000 \\
001 \\
011 \\
010 \\
110 \\
111 \\
101 \\
100
\end{array}$$

Find all such orders, and investigate relations between them.

3. Investigate the set of triangles which have perimeters of 12 units.

4. The diagram shows a member of the set of quadrilaterals whose

171

sides are tangents to a given circle. Investigate.

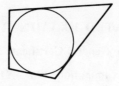

5. Write an essay on *Probability*.

The paper is clearly of great interest but it can be argued that it is inappropriate to try to test this kind of skill or ability under examinations conditions at all. Rather it would be preferable to acknowledge that this is a *component* we wish to include in assessment, but that this component should be assessed by course work rather than by examination.

There are advantages to this: students can be asked during their course to carry out a number of investigations and for assessment purposes to submit for scrutiny by the 'examiner' one or two, or any specified number of pieces of work *of their own choice*. This puts the onus on the student to try to assess in which pieces of work that he has done, he is demonstrating his abilities to the fullest; and we arrive very much at the criteria of *self-understanding*. On the other hand there is, after the first year or so, ample opportunity for plagiarism, particularly if members of staff change! Nevertheless I feel that it is a risk worth taking, and that evaluation of a course should include an examination which would largely test certain knowledge and skills, together with a certain amount of course work chosen and submitted by the student himself for the purposes of assessment. Finally there should be a component referring to attitudes to work, to conscientiousness, enthusiasm, regularity in completion of assignments, relationships with others.

The teacher's record book therefore will include all the following components:

(*a*) Record of exercises completed and understandings gained.

(*b*) Record of practical work done in groups or otherwise with letter grades for neatness, presentation, and accuracy.

(*c*) Record of achievement in tests and examinations.

(*d*) Record of investigations completed, some of which will be selected by the student for incorporation into his assessment.

Such a record will enable a teacher to complete with confidence a profile on each student such as that suggested on page 153. This not only gives a clearer picture of a student's ability at any given time, but it enables a teacher to talk knowledgeably with parents about each child's progress, to counsel students about their future, and to write recommendations for places of further education or future employers.

Summary
Evaluation involves

(*a*) observing and helping students as they work;

(*b*) assigning, directing, and evaluating student written work, exercises, reports, projects and investigations;

(*c*) constructing, administering, marking and evaluating tests and examinations;

(*d*) recording evaluations, interpreting them and incorporating them in a profile of student achievement and ability;

(*e*) reflecting upon the interaction between teacher and student so that improvements can be made in the teaching process.

In short, evaluation is a continuing process which aims on the one hand at ensuring the continuing progress of each individual student and compiling a suitable record of that progress, and on the other at constantly improving the performance of the teacher himself.

Appendix. A Mathematics Laboratory

A suggested layout is given in Fig. 117, followed by details of construction.

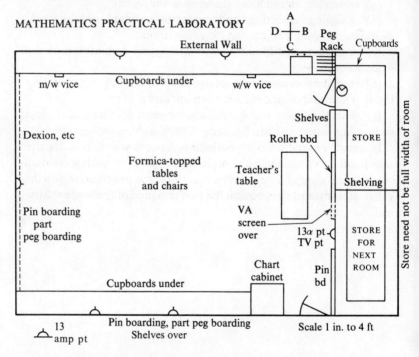

Fig. 117. Mathematics practical laboratory.

Side benches

Side benches 2 ft 10 in (86 cm) high × 2 ft (61 cm) wide with Iroko top, beach underframe to standard bench design.

Cupboard units and drawer units built in below side benches, including one cupboard of 4 ft (122 cm) for long apparatus, e.g. surveying apparatus, etc. flush-fitting removable masking panels in blank spaces.

Sinks

(*a*) 1 *Belfast* sink 24 in × 18 in × 10 in.

(*b*) Water taps swan neck laboratory type, hot tap to be mounted on R.H.S. All taps to be *Vultex* make in black varecoat finish.

General

(*a*) Means of ventilating room when blackout is in use.

(*b*) Shelving for books where convenient.

(*c*) Pinboarding with some peg boarding where possible.

(*d*) Lighting in laboratory and store to be fluorescent strip lighting to provide lighting intensity on all working surfaces according to Ministry's recommendation.

(*e*) Roller blinds running in grooves of adequate width to provide blackout to all windows in the laboratory.

Wall A (external wall)

(*a*) Standard side bench with 3 cupboard units and 3 drawer units and one 4 ft cupboard unit under.

(*b*) 4 ft *Belfast* sink unit with draining board and hot and cold taps positioned as shown on the plan.

(*c*) Peg drainer 2 ft high and 1 ft 9 in wide and paper towel dispenser on return wall at end of draining board.

(*d*) *Record* 6 in clamp-on woodwork vice and 3 in metalwork vice positioned as shown on the plan.

(*e*) Two 13 amp power points over bench positioned as shown on the plan.

Wall B

(*a*) Roller type blackboard, one section squared 9 ft 0 in high and 6 ft 4½ in wide, visual aid screen mounted over blackboard.

(*b*) 4 rows of 3 ft × 8 in ×¾ in blockboard shelves, mahogany-lipped mounted on two 6 ft lengths of industrial quality *Tebrax* on wall at side of blackboard remote from wall C.

(*c*) One television point on side of blackboard.

(*d*) One 13 amp power point on same side of blackboard as television point.

(*e*) 6 ft × 3 ft pinboarding by side of blackboard positioned as shown on plan.

(*f*) Electric clock with sweep second hand above store room door.

Wall C (Internal wall)

(*a*) Standard side bench with 3 cupboard units and 3 drawer units under. Chart cabinet approx. 3 ft 6 in × 2 ft 6 in × 2 ft 10 in high, containing 6 long drawers to hold wall charts fitted between bench and door.

(*b*) 4 ft high pinboarding along whole length of wall above bench.

(*c*) *Tebrax* channels at 3 ft centres from top of pinboarding to ceiling complete with brackets to take one 9 in shelf.

(*d*) Two 13 amp power points on wall over bench, positioned as shown on plan.

Wall D

(*a*) Strip of *Dexion* or similar material let into ceiling about 4 in from the wall along the whole width of the room. Length of *Dexion* strip or similar material let into the floor along whole width of the wall about 4 in from the wall. Six lengths of *Dexion* or similar material for vertical erection between these two strips.

(*b*) Pinboarding with some pegboarding along whole width of room extending from height of about 3 ft to about 7 ft.

(*c*) One 13 amp power point fixed centrally below pinboarding.

Store room
Walls B, C, and D

Adjustable shelving on 6 ft 6 in industrial quality *Tebrax* channels spaced at 2 ft centres to accommodate 6 rows of 9 in wide softwood shelving.

Wall A

Whitewood cupboard approx. 3 ft high along whole width of wall.

MINIMUM AREA – 720 sq. ft *plus* Store room

[Details taken from *Mathematics laboratories in schools*, prepared for the Mathematical Association and printed by G. Bell & Sons Ltd.]

Index

Abelian group, 24
ability
    differences in, 72–7
    profile of, 153–4
accuracy, 40, 43
addition
    laws of, 24
    of signed numbers, 3–4, 135–6
algebra
    basic, 53–4
    Boolean, 22, 35–8
analysis
    of examination paper, 166–8
    of *Making Mathematics*, 65–70
    of *SMP* course, 62–5
    of syllabus, 59–62
angle, trisection of, 105
approximation
    in calculations, 51–3
    in measurement, 43–4
area, 48, 105
arrow diagrams, 30–3
associativity, 24
attitudes, 2, 18

blackboard, 132
Bloom, Prof. B.S., 162
Boolean algebra, 22, 35–8

calculating machines, 52, 146
cassettes, 8 mm film loop, 127
circle, 48
    unit, 98–9, 101
classroom organisation, 122–3
commutativity, 24
computers, 38–40
concepts, 2
    formation of, 83–5
content, 1–2, 21–70
cosine, 97–9
daily lesson plan, 109–10
    evaluation of, 151–2
deduction, 14
definitions, 80
    of integers as ordered pairs, 92
Descartes, 16
determinants, 94–5

Dienes' multibase equipment, 133–4
    logic blocks, 134
directed numbers
    addition of, 3–4, 135–6
    multiplication of, 88–92
discrimination, 166–8
displacements, 99
display boards, 131
domino technique, 116–17

elevations, plans and, 45–6, 137–8
elimination, 93
envelopes, 140
equations, 53–6, 92–5
equivalence, 23–4, 30–1, 36
Euclid, 95–6
Euler, 17–18
evaluation, 1, 4, 151–73

films, 125–6
filmstrips, 126
flash cards, 117–8
flow charts, 38–40
    for adding with hand calculator,
        52
    of concept formation, 83
    for controlling progress, 87
    using determinants, 95
    of problem solving, 41, 83
    of process of measurement, 42
    for slide rule, 51
    of teaching process, 1
    for testing, 168
functions, 31–4, 100–4

games, 141–3
geometry
    Euclidean, 57–8
    and sets, 22, 26–30
geo-strips, 134–5
goals of education, 1, 6–10, 19
graphs, 31–3, 54–7, 90–1, 93
group
    structure of, 24
    symmetry, orders of, 27
group work, 74–5, 119–21

hand calculators, 52, 146
Hogben, Lancelot, 16

identity element, 24
instructional file, 105
inverse element, 24
investigations, 14–15, 77–9
isometric projection, 45
isomorphism, 25

kite, 26–8
Konigsberg bridge problem, 17–18

laboratory, mathematics, 147–9, 174–6
latitude, 49–50, 137
library, mathematics, 149–50
lesson planning, 107–10
lesson, types of, 110–22
logarithms, 25, 102–4
  use in slide rule, 144–5
logic, 18, 22, 35–8
longitude, 49–50, 137

Making Mathematics, 65–70
mapping, 31–4
materials, 1, 4, 124–50
mathematical model, 17
mathematics laboratory, 147–9, 174–6
mathematics library, 149–50
matrix, 94
measurement, 41–4, 61–70, 119–21
memory work, 86
method, 1, 4, 13–14, 107–23
models, 133–41
multiplication, laws of, 24

Napier's rods (bones), 145–6
nets, of cuboid, 45–6
nodes, 18
numbers
  in computers, 40
  various sets of, 22–3
number theory, 21–5, 61–70

objectives
  of mathematics teaching, 11–20
  in test construction, 161–6
  utilitarian, 41–57

Pacioli, 16
parallelograms, 26–8
pattern
  in concept formation, 84
  use in directed numbers, 89–91

and periodic change, 100
as part of problem solving, 80–1
in teaching logarithms, 103
Perigal's dissection, 97
plans and elevations, 45–6, 137–8
Polya, 41
probability, 34
problem solving, 40–1, 59–60, 79–83,
  121, 162–5.
profile of child ability, 153–4
programmed textbook, 76–7
progress, control of, 87–8
projector
  opaque, 130–1
  overhead, 127–30, 139
pyramids, 136
Pythagoras' theorem, 95–7

quadrilaterals, 26–8

radian measure, 100–1
ratio, 97–8
rectangle, 26–7
Regiomontanus, 16
record book, 172–3
relations, 22, 30–4
  and graphs, 61–70
reliability, 159
rhombus, 26–8

scales, sliding, 3–4, 135–6, 144–5
scheme of work, 107
School Mathematics Project (SMP),
  62–5
School Mathematics Study Group
  (SMSG), 162–3
sets, 21–40, 58–9
shape, and measurement, 61–70
signed numbers
  addition of, 3–4, 135–6
  multiplication of, 88–92
simultaneous equations, 54–6, 92–5
sine, 97–9
skills
  as educational objective, 2, 9
  learning of, 85–6
slide rule, 144–5
sphere, 48–50
square, 26–8
statistics, 22, 34
Stevinus, 16
strategy, 1–4, 72–106
structure
  of course work, 59–70

of group, 24
substitution, 93
syllabus, 21–71
   evaluation of, 151–73
symbols, development of, 16

tangent, 97–9
tape recorders, 126–7
teaching process, 1–5
television, 126
tessellations, 57–8
tests, 157–72
textbook, 62–70, 124–5

three dimensional objects, 44–6
topics, 74–6
triangle, 46–9, 57–8
   area of, 105
trigonometry, 97–101
truth tables, 35–8

unit circle, 98–9, 101
unit plans, 108

validity, 159
vectors, 29–30
Vieta, 16